SHC

POCKET BOOK

松涛館小本

KEN LYONS

拳

FIRST EDITION
2006

Zanchin Press
Uxbridge Middlesex England

CW01432405

Note for Librarians: A cataloguing record for this book is available from Library and Archives
Canada at www.collectionscanada.ca/amicus/index-e.html

ISBN 1-4120-9342-2

TRAFFORD
P U B L I S H I N G™

Offices in Canada, USA, Ireland and UK

Book sales for North America and international:
Trafford Publishing, 6E–2333 Government St.,
Victoria, BC V8T 4P4 CANADA
phone 250 383 6864 (toll-free 1 888 232 4444)
fax 250 383 6804; email to orders@trafford.com

Book sales in Europe:
Trafford Publishing (UK) Limited, 9 Park End Street, 2nd Floor
Oxford, UK OX1 1HH UNITED KINGDOM
phone +44 (0)1865 722 113 (local rate 0845 230 9601)
facsimile +44 (0)1865 722 868; info.uk@trafford.com

Order online at:
trafford.com/06-1096

10 9 8 7 6 5 4 3 2 1

Introduction
(Hajimeni)

はじめに

The Shotokan Pocket Book is a compilation of the translation of Karateka Terminology and other Japanese words and phrases into English. This book has been written to assist students of Karate-Do and to supplement their training and learning processes. Both junior and senior Karateka should find this book useful.

In compiling this book, the primary objective has been to provide a comprehensive reference book that lists the various Japanese terms, commands and expressions that are used when training in the dojo and when taking part in competition. Sections 2 to 19 are devoted to this.

Section 1 explains the general rules of pronunciation of Japanese for the English speaking tongue. It is important to spend time understanding the basic principles which should assist students to read and annunciate Japanese words correctly.

Sections 20, 21 and 22 contain the Dojo Kun, the 20 Precepts of Gichin Funakoshi and Japanese numbers from one to one hundred respectively for quick reference.

Whilst the terms used are primarily the same for all of the popular Japanese Karate styles there are some variations and differences in spelling and pronunciation. This book attempts to take account of this fact and includes the most popular alternatives where applicable. Whilst this book will therefore be useful to Karateka of all styles it focuses on the Shotokan style and therefore Section 14 contains the 26 Shotokan Kata. In addition, this section contains other terms that are used in relation with Kata and one or two Kata performed by other styles which are of particular interest to Shotokan Karateka.

Acknowledgments
(Shaji)
謝辞

I would like to thank Kyoshi Mick Dewey, Chief Instructor of the Shotokan of England Karate Union (SEKU), for his advice and encouragement in the early stages of compiling the data for this book and for being a great mentor.

I would also like to thank Sensei Frank Hatton for introducing me to SEKU, for being a ferocious taskmaster in the Dojo and a good friend outside the Dojo.

When I first began training and practicing the art of Karate-Do I was foolish enough to think it was merely a way of keeping fit while also learning a form of self defence. For me, Karate training and development has been, and will continue to be, a journey that has changed me in many ways. I found Karate challenging and the process of confronting and overcoming those challenges has been rewarding and enlightening and I have benefited both physically and mentally from the experiences. The journey continues and I am indebted to Karate-Do and the many characters I have met and friends I have made along the way.

Guide To This Book
(Honsho No Tsukaikata)

本 書 の 使 い 方

The book is subdivided into sections containing areas of interest in order for students to track down what they are looking for quickly and within each section the entries (Japanese words and phrases) are listed in alphabetical order and in bold uppercase type. Where there is an alternative spelling (and subsequent alternative pronunciation) this appears in bold uppercase also and in brackets immediately after the word.

Each entry is followed by the English translation. Where the translation into English can be expressed as more that one similar word or phrase, these are separated by commas.

Occasionally, an entry will have more than one (different) meaning. These are listed and numbered e.g. **(1)** and **(2).**

Any other additional information follows on in italics type face. Note that, where applicable, this will include alternative names, words or terms for the entry in Japanese. For example "**EMPI –** Elbow. *Also referred to as ""Hiji"*".

The definitions of the most commonly used terms used in Shotokan appear in bold to help the reader to identify them quickly.

For suggestion of words or phrases to be included in future editions of this book please contact:
zanchin.press@btinternet.com.

Contents
(Mokuji)

目 次

1

Japanese Pronunciation (Nihongo No Hatsuon)

This section provides an introduction to spoken Japanese and general guidance for reading Japanese words that have been transliterated into written English and the correct pronunciations.

日本語の発音

By taking the time to learn basic Japanese pronunciation we expand our knowledge and understanding of the culture that gave birth to the art we practice and in doing so, we also show our respect for its origins and those willing to share its secrets.

It is extremely difficult for westerners to learn how to read and write Japanese, however, at the basic level it is a relatively easy to learn to speak the language correctly, particularly when it is translated phonetically into English.

It is important for Karateka to take the time to learn basic pronunciation in order to speak and understand the short phrases that are used in the dojo. This short section should provide some guidance.

Most Karateka do not study Japanese and learn the terms without full appreciation of the correct Japanese pronunciation. The Japanese spoken in most dojos has been passed down from student to student and simplified for our native tongue. Whilst it is good to become acquainted with the correct pronunciation, in practice it is important that you follow the standards of your club so that you are understood in the dojo.

To western ears, spoken Japanese may sound abrupt and monotonous. This is for two reasons. Firstly, the syllables of a word are all given equal speed and length. Secondly, words within a sentence are all give equal stress. The fact that each word and the syllables of each word are given the same amount of importance prevents the rise and fall of voice intonation that affects western languages.

Examples:

	English Pronunciation	Japanese Pronunciation
Okinawa	Okin AAwa	O–ki –na–wa
Yokohama	Yoko HAAma	Yo–ko–ha–ma
Kimono	Kim HOEno	Ki–mo–no

As the above examples, Japanese is essentially syllabic; which means that words are broken into individual syllables. This is reasonably simple for westerners to understand but the key to reading and speaking the language is the understanding of the correct pronunciation of vowels.

There are many different ways people have of writing down Japanese words using the Roman alphabet, none of which are entirely correct but here are five general (root) sounds to pronunciation or short vowels.

As you explore and familiarize yourself with the words and Karate–Do terminology in this book, you are recommended to use the following vowel guide to aid you in your pronunciation. Japanese syllables consist of a vowel alone, a combination of vowels + consonants or consonant + glide + vowel.

Short Vowel Pronunciation

Japanese has five vowels· a, i, u, c, and o when Romanized. The vowels are short and clipped when compared to English. This is because there is a distinction between long and short vowel sounds; short vowel sounds count as one syllable, and long sounds count as two. The pronunciation is the same but the sound is held longer.

a = Pronounced: ah (as in: cart or bar)
e = Pronounced: eh (as in: net or bed)
i = Pronounced: ee (as in: tea or feet)
o = Pronounced: oh (as in: no or note)
u = Pronounced: oo (as in: put or foot but not boot)

When a word ends in a short vowel, the vowel is shortened still further and cut off sharply. For Example "osu" is pronounced "os" with a very short, sharp "u" on the end. Most non-Japanese people have difficulty pronouncing this so it is usual for "osu" to be spoken as "oss"'. Similarly "tsuki" should be "ts(u)k(i)" which should be pronounced somewhere between "tsuki" and "tsk".

Long Vowel (Double Vowel) Pronunciation

Long vowels are pronounced like the short vowels but held for twice as long. Care should be taken to pronounce them as a continuous sound, equal in value to two identical short vowels.
In Romanization of the double vowel sounds, the *best* way to indicate these sounds would be to have the bar over top the vowel. However, due to the limited ASCII character set which doesn't have all these vowels, this is not always possible or convenient. Therefore the alternate is to use a double vowel, for example "Jiin" is used in this book. However, in order to avoid the obvious pitfall of mispronouncing the long o represented by "oo" it is shown as "ou" to assist with the correct pronunciation. Similarly the long e is represented by "ei" rather than "ee".

      Long a is written aa or ā   (as in: dr<u>a</u>ma)
      Long e is written ei or ē   (as in: M<u>ay</u>)
      Long i is written ii or ī   (as in: kn<u>ee</u>)
      Long o is written ou or ō   (as in: <u>ow</u>n)
      Long u is written uu or ū   (as in: c<u>oo</u>l)

In addition, there are also other long vowel sounds usually written as two different vowels.

      ai   =   Pronounced: eye (Example: al<u>i</u>ve)
      ae   =   Pronounced: ayee (Example: d<u>ay</u>)
      au   =   Pronounced: ow (Example: <u>ou</u>t)

Syllables: Consonant + Vowel combinations

Most of the sounds in the language are made by adding a consonant in front of the vowel.

ka	ki	ku	ke	ko
sa	shi	su	se	so
ta	chi	tsu	te	to
na	ni	nu	ne	no
ha	hi	fu	he	ho
ma	mi	mu	me	mo
ya		yu		yo
ra	ri	ru	re	ro
wa				(w)o

Modified Syllables: Consonant + Vowel combinations

ga	gi	gu	ge	go
za	ji	zu	ze	zo
da	ji	zu	de	do
ba	bi	bu	be	bo
pa	pi	pu	pe	po

There is some difficulty that comes with the "Ra" group as the Japanese do not have "r" or "l" sound. Their "r" sound is a combination of the two there "ra" should sound a little like "rla".

5

Combined Syllables (Consonant + Glide + Vowel)

These are pronounced cleanly as a single sound.

kya	kyu	kyo
sha	shu	sho
cha	chu	cho
nya	nyu	nyo
hya	hyu	hyo
mya	myu	myo
rya	ryu	ryo
gya	gyu	gyo
ja	ju	jo
bya	byu	byo
pya	pyu	pyo

Examples:

gya	=	Pronounced: geea
kya	=	Pronounced: key–are
gyu	=	Pronounced: gee–oo
sho	=	Pronounced: show
myo	=	Pronounced: my–owe
cha	=	Pronounced: char
chi	=	Pronounced: chee (Example: cheese)
tsu	=	Pronounced: dzoo or tzoo
ite	=	Pronounced: eetay

Consonants

Most consonants are pronounced as they are in English. A few that may need clarifying are listed below.

b = pronounced as in bed
d = pronounced as in dog
f = pronounced as in far
h = pronounced as in help
j = pronounced as in jar (and a d sound before l as in dog)
k = pronounced as in king
m = pronounced as in mother
n = pronounced as in nice
p = pronounced as in pig
s = pronounced as in see
t = pronounced: as in top
w = pronounced as in wall
y = pronounced as in yard
z = pronounced as in haze

g = pronounced as in go (beginning of word) everywhere else it is pronounced like "ng" in ring.

r = pronounced with the tongue more or less in the position for "l" but the tongue does not touch the front of the mouth and the sound "rolled". Also "r" is pronounced a bit like a "d" in the middle of a word.

"y" can be used as a vowel as well as consonant. When used as a constant some words are written with a "g" in front of the "y" to indicate that the "y" is not to be taken as a vowel but the `g' is not pronounced. For example "gyaku" (opposite, reverse) and pronounced "yak(u)" and not "ee-ak(u)". That said you will be excused for following the pronunciation used as your own dojo.

ch = pronounced as in touch
sh = pronounced as in sheep
ts = pronounced as in hat stand. This sound is shortened to a "z" when not sounded alone as in tsuzi.

Double consonants

Doubled consonants are usually in the form of "tt", "pp", "kk", "ss" and are sounded with a short pause between the letters. Therefore "tettsui" is pronounced "tet-tsui" and not "tetzui".

Additional Pronunciation

The pronunciation of most consonants are similar to English, however, b, d, g k, p, s, t and z are all pronounced without fully exhaling thus producing a more clipped sound.

The "u" is frequently mute in Japanese except where it is the initial syllable. In particular when "u" follows an "s" it is not articulated. Foe Example dare "desu ka" (who is it?) becomes "dare des'ka" and "mokuso" (empty mind) becomes "mok'so".

In some works "i" disappears. For example "shi" often becomes "sh" as in "deshita" which is pronounced "desh'ta"

The "fu" sound is pronounced halfway between "fu" and "hu". This is achieved with a gentle breath between the slightly parted lips.

Translation

The translations of Japanese karate terms into English are more a description of the action rather that a strict translation of the words. In this book, the strict translation, where appropriate will precede the description of the actions. For example, "oi zuki" (the action of stepping forward and delivering a punch with the leading side of the body) translates as chase "oi" and stab/thrust "zuki". Stepping forward and punching is the description of the action.

2

Punching Techniques (Zuki Waza)

This section contains terminology relating to single punches, jabs and other offensive techniques executed with a closed hand or clenched fist.

突
技

AGE ZUKI (AGE TSUKI) – Rising punch. *Executed by extending arm downwards and bringing it up with arm straight, striking with the back of fist. As performed in the Kata Empi.*

CHOKU ZUKI (CHOKU TSUKI) – Straight punch, Static punch. *Executed from Hachiji Dachi. Also referred to as Kara Zuki.*

CHUDAN CHOKU ZUKI – Straight punch to the chest/mid–section.

CHUDAN ZUKI (CHUDAN TSUKI) – Middle level, chest, mid–section punch. *This is a punch to the mid–section of the opponent's body.*

GEDAN CHOKU ZUKI – Straight punch to the groin.

GEDAN NI OSHIDASU – Thrust downwards.

GEDAN OSHIDASHI – Low level thrust.

GEDAN ZUKI (GEDAN TSUKI) – Downward punch, low level punch. *This is a punch to the lower section/groin. As performed in the Kata Hangetsu.*

GYAKU ZUKI NO TSUKOMI – Lunging reverse, or back–hand punch. *The punch corresponds to the opposite side of the body as the leading leg. This is a Wado Ryu Term.*

GYAKU ZUKI (GYAKU TSUKI) – Reverse punch. *The basic reverse punch is practiced from Zenkutsu Dachi, twisting the hips from a 45° angle to front, square with hips and shoulder. Opposite legs forward to hand that is punching.*

HIRAKEN ZUKI – Four knuckle fist straight punch.

HITOSASHI IPPON KEN – Forefinger knuckle. *Also referred to as Ippon Ken.*

HITOSASHIYUBI IPPON KEN – Forefinger fist. *Also referred to as Ippon Ken.*

IPPON KEN – One knuckle fist. *Striking with the second knuckle of an extended index finger of the clenched fist. Used to attack vulnerable and vital points. As performed in the Kata Hangetsu. Also called Ippon Naki Daki Ken.*
IPPON KEN ZUKI – One knuckle fist straight punch.

IPPON ZUKI (IPPON TSUKI) – One finger thrust. *The index finger is extended and all other fingers and the thumb are in the closed position.*

JODAN AGE ZUKI – Upper, high level rising punch. *As performed in the Kata Empi.*

JODAN CHOKU ZUKI – Upper, high level straight punch.

JODAN OSHIDASHI – Upper, high level thrust.

JODAN URA ZUKI – Upper, high level close punch. *An upper cut punch used at close range. As performed in the Kata Tekki Shodan.*

JUN ZUKI – Spring punch, corresponding punch. *Stepping punch where the punch corresponds with the same side of the body as the leading leg. The Wado Ryu term for Oi Zuki.*

JUN ZUKI NO TSUKOMI – Stepping lunging punch. *The punch corresponds with the same side of the body as the leading leg. This is a Wado Ryu Term.*

KEN – Fist, closed hand technique. *Also means 'to hook', 'sword', 'tendon', 'active condition', 'alert state'.*

KENTSUI – Iron fist, hammer fist, mace–hand. *The attack is delivered with the bottom of the fist. Use to attack head, shoulders, elbow joints, ribs. Can also be used as a block. As performed in the Kata Heian Shodan. Also referred to as Tettsui and Shutsui.*

KAGI ZUKI (KAGE TSUKI) – Hook punch. *Executed with elbow bent at a 90° angle and forearm parallel to your body, the arm is tilted slightly downwards in the Mizue Nagare (Flowing Water) position. As performed in the Kata Tekki Shodan and Heian Godan.*

KAKIWAKE OROSU – Down ward thrust.

KARA ZUKI (KARA TSUKI) – Straight punch. *Executed from Hachiji Dachi. Also referred to as Choku Zuki.*

KIZAMI – Jab, snap.

KIZAMI ZUKI (KIZAMI TSUKI) – Jabbing punch, snap punch, lunge punch. *Executed from Zenkutsu Dachi with hips and shoulders at a 45° angle and with the punch being executed on the same side of the body as the leading leg.*

KOHO ZUKI AGE (KOHO TSUKI AGE) – Back direction rising punch. As performed in the Kata Heian Godan.

MAWASHI ZUKI (MAWASHI TSUKI) – Roundhouse punch. *Executed by swinging fist in a wide arc from hip to target and making contact with the side of the body.*

MIGIKAE ZUKI (MIGIKAE TSUKI) – Jab punch.

NAGASHI ZUKI (NAGASHI TSUKI) – Flowing punch. *Cross counter punch with the leading hand. Similar to Oi Zuki; can be used either moving forward or back while hips are at 45° angle.*

NAKADAKA IPPON KEN – Middle finger one knuckle fist. *Also referred to as Nakayubi Ippon Ken.*

NAKAYUBI PPON KEN – Middle finger one knuckle fist. *Also referred to as Nakadaka Ippon Ken.*

NAKADAKA KEN – Middle finger knuckle fist.

ONI KEN – Extended knuckle fist.

OI ZUKI (OI TSUKI) – Lunge punch, stepping punch. Translated as chasing thrust. Executed by stepping forward into Zenkutsu Dachi with hips and shoulders square to the front. The punch is executed on the same side of the body as the stepping leg.

OTOSHI ZUKI – Downward Punch, dropping punch. *As performed in the Kata Kanku Dai.*

OYAYUBI IPPON KEN – Thumb knuckle.

SANREN ZUKI – Flowing punch.

SEIKEN – Straight fist, normal fist, fore fist, regular fist. Striking with the knuckles of the index and middle fingers of the clenched fist.

SEIKEN ZUKI (SEIKEN TSUKI) – Normal/straight/fore/regular fist thrust punch.

SHI KIN KEN – Four raised knuckles.

SHITTSUI – Knee hammer.

SHUTSUI (SHUTTSUI) – Iron fist, hammer fist, mace–hand. *The attack is delivered with the bottom of the fist. Use to attack head, shoulders, elbow joints, ribs. Can also be used as a block. As performed in the Kata Heian Shodan. Also referred to as Kentsui and Tettsui.*

TATE ZUKI (TATE TSUKI) – Vertical fist punch. *The fist is rotated at 90 degrees with the palm along a vertical plane.*

TETSUI (TETTSUI) – Iron fist, hammer fist, mace–hand. The attack is delivered with the bottom of the fist. Use to attack head, shoulders, elbow joints, ribs. Can also be used as a block. As performed in the Kata Heian Shodan. Also referred to as Kentsui and Shutsui.

TETSUI UCHI (TETTSUI UCHI) – Hammer fist strike. A *strike using the bottom of the fist. As performed in the Kata Heian Shodan. Also called Kentsui Uchi.*

TOBI–ZUKI – Jumping punch.

TOBOKOMI ZUKI – Snap punch, jumping thrust punch. *Using the leading hand.*

TSUKI AGE – Swinging punch, rising punch.

TSUKIDASHI – Thrust.

TSUKI (ZUKI) – Thrusting punch.

TSUKI UCHI (ZUKI UCHI) – Thrusting strike, punching strike.

TSUKI WAZA (ZUKI WAZA) – Punching techniques.

UKE ZUKI – Block punch.

URA – Back fist, upper cut. *Also means 'reverse', 'back', 'rear'.*

URA ZUKI (URA TSUKI) – Close punch, upper cut. *Used at short distance, short punch with wrist facing up and the wrist not rotated. As performed in the Kata Tekki Shodan. Also referred to as Staz Zuki.*

YUMI ZUKI (YUMI TSUKI) – Bow punch, bow drawing punch. The opponents hand is pulled forward as the punch is executed. *As performed in the Kata Jion (final move).*

ZUKI (TSUKI) – Punch, thrusting punch.

ZUKI WAZA (TSUKI WAZA) – Punching techniques.

3

Two–Handed & Multiple Punching Techniques (Morote Zuki Waza To Ren Zuki Waza)

This section contains terminology relating two handed or multiple punches, jabs and other offensive techniques executed simultaneously or consecutively with a closed hand or clenched fist.

諸手突き技と連突き技

AWASE ZUKI (AWASE TSUKI) – U–punch. *Two simultaneous punches, upper fist Jodan Gyaku Zuki and lower fist Chudan Ura Zuki. As performed in the Kata Nijushiho. Also referred to as Morote Zuki.*

CURI ZUKI (CURI TSUKI) – Double punch, freestyle combination punch.

DAN ZUKI (DAN TSUKI) – Consecutive punch. Punching repeatedly with the same hand.

HEIKO TATE ZUKI – Parallel vertical fist punch. *As performed in the Kata Gojushiho Dai.*

HEIKO URA ZUKI – Parallel close punch. *As performed in the Kata Bassai Sho.*

HEIKO ZUKI (HEIKO TSUKI) – Parallel punch, double punch. *Two simultaneous punches side by side. As performed in the Kata Bassai Sho and Meikyo.*

HASAMI TETTSUI UCHI – Scissor bottom fist strike. Both bottom fists execute a scissor strike in to the sides of the attacker's body.

HASAMI ZUKI (HASAMI TSUKI) – Scissors punch. *Two simultaneous punches coming out from the hips in a wide arc to target both sides of the opponent's body. As performed in the Kata Chinte.*

MOROTE KOHO TSUKI AGE – Augmented swinging punch to the rear. *As performed in the Kata Heian Godan.*

MOROTE YOKO KEN ATE – Double handed side fist strike.

MOROTE ZUKI (MOROTE TSUKI) – Two–hand punch. Augmented punch, double fist punch, U punch. *Punching with both fists simultaneously. Also referred to as Awase Zuki. As performed in the Kata Tekki Shodan.*

NIHON ZUKI – Two consecutive punches from alternate hands.

REN ZUKI (REN TSUKI) – **Alternate punching, consecutive punching.** *Punching with the left and right fists alternately, two or three times.*

RYOKEN – Both fists.

RYOWAN – Both arms.

SANBON ZUKI (SANBON TSUKI) – **Three consecutive punches, triple punch.** *For example Oi Zuki Jodan, followed by a slight pause then, Chudan Gyaku Zuki, immediately followed by Chudan Choku Zuki.*

SOKUMEN MOROTE ZUKI – Side double punch.

TETSUI HASAMI UCHI – **Hammer fist scissors strike, bottom fist scissor strike, side double punch.** *As performed in the Kata Bassai Dai.*

YAMA ZUKI (YAMA TSUKI) – **Mountain wide U punch.** *A wide U shaped dual punch. Two simultaneous punches, upper fist Jodan and lower fist Chudan Ura Zuki. As performed in the Kata Bassai Dai.*

YOKO UDE HASAMI – Side forearm scissors.

4

Open Hand Striking Techniques (Kaishu Uchi Wasa)

This section contains terminology relating to single, two handed or multiple offensive striking techniques executed with an open hand.

開
手
打
ち
技

HAISHU (**HAISHO, HAESHU**) – Back of flat hand, back–hand. *Striking with the back of a flat hand. Used to attack the face or ribs.*

HAISHU AGE UCHI – Back hand rising strike. *As performed in the Kata Nijushiho.*

HAISHU JUJI UKE – Backhand cross block.

HAISHU UCHI (HAISHO UCHI) – Back–hand strike. *A strike with the back of the flat hand where the hand and fingers are straight.*

HAITO – Ridge–hand, ridge of the hand. *The thumb is extended across the palm of the flat hand towards the little finger and the base of the index finger is used as the striking edge. Used to attack face and ribs.*

HAITO IPPON KEN – Ridge–hand one–knuckle fist.

HAITO UCHI – Ridge–hand strike.

HIRABASAMI – Claw–hand.

HIRA HASAMI – Flat scissors. *Also referred to as Koko.*

HIRAKEN – Flat fist strike, fore knuckle fist strike. *Fingers tips are bent to touch the palm. The back of the fingers (between the fist and second knuckles are used to attack vulnerable and vital points (e.g. between the nose and upper lip, solar plexus and temples.*

HIRAKEN ZUKI (HIRAKEN TSUKI) – Flat fist punch, fore–knuckle fist, back fist fingers strike. *Tips of the fingers are bent to touch the palm.*

HIRA NUKITE – Level spear hand or level piercing hand. The palm is facing down.

HITOSASHI IPPON KEN – Forefinger knuckle.

IPPON KEN FURI OTOSHI – One knuckle fist circular drop. *As performed in the Kata Chinte.*

IPPON KEN GYAKU FURI OTOSHI – One knuckle fist reversed circular drop. *As performed in the Kata Chinte.*

JODAN SHUTO UCHI – Upper, high level knife–hand strike. *As performed in the Kata Heian Yondan.*

KAISHO (KAISHU) – Open hand, open hand techniques. *This is a general term for strikes and blocks that are executed the open palm or where the fist is not fully clenched.*

KAISHU UCHI (KAISHO UCHI) – Open hand strike/s.

KAKUTO – Bent wrist. *The wrist is bent and the attack is delivered with the back of the wrist punching arm or armpit.*

KAKUTO UCHI – Bent wrist strike, wrist joint strike. *Also referred to as Ko Uchi.*

KEIKO – Joined fingertips, chicken head hand.

KEITO – Chicken head wrist. *The hand is bent outwards, with the thumb bent and the fingers curled. The attack is delivered with base of the thumb to the throat or arm pit. Also used as a block. As performed in the Kata Unsu and Gojushiho Dai.*

KEITO UCHI – Chicken head strike.

KOKEN – Chicken head. *Also means wrist joint and bent wrist.*

KOKO:
(1) – Tiger mouth. *Open hand with fingers together and thumb position to form a 'C' shape with the index finger. Used for attack throat or Adam's Apple.*
(2) – Here.

KOKO UCHI – Tiger mouth strike. Executed by striking with the area between the thumb and index finger.

KUMADE:
(1) – Bear hand. *Fingers and thumb are bent to touch the palm of the hand in a claw like fashion. Used mainly for attacking the ears and face.*
(2) – Rake, fork.

KUMADE UCHI – Bear hand strike.

MOROTE SEIRYUTO UCHI – Two handed ox–jaw strike. *Generally used against the collar bones.*

NIHON NUKITE – Split finger strike, two finger spear–hand strike, two finger stabbing attack. *Strike is executed using the tips of the index finger and middle finger held apart. Used to attack the eyes. As performed in the Kata Chinte.*

NIHON ZUKI (NIHON TSUKI) – Two finger thrust. *The index finger and middle finger are extended and thumb is used to hold down the ring and little finger in the closed position.*

NISHI KEN – One finger spear strike. *Also referred to as Ippon Nukite.*

NUKITE – Spear–hand. *Translation is 'penetrating hand'. Strike is executed using the tips of the fingers. See also Shihon Nukite and Nihon Nukite.*

NUKITE UCHI – Spear–hand strike. *Translation is 'penetrating hand strike'. Strike is executed using the tips of the fingers.*

SEIRYUTO – Ox jaw hand, bull jaw hand. *A hand technique delivered with the base of the Shuto (knife–hand) as a block or an attack to the collar bone. As performed in the Kata Hangetsu.*

SEIRYUTO ZUKI – Ox jaw hand punch.

SHIHON NUKITE – Spear–hand, four finger spear–hand strike. *Translation is 'penetrating hand'. Four fingers held tightly together and the strike is executed*

by using the tips of first three fingers. As performed in the Kata Heian Nidan.

SHIHONZUKI (SHIHON TSUKI) – Four finger thrust.

SHOTAI (SHOTEI, SHOTE) (TAISHO) – Palm of Hand, palm heel. *The palm of the hand when the fingers are drawn back.*

SHUTO – **Knife–hand, sword–hand, knife–edge.** *Flat hand with thumb and little finger pressing fingers together. Used on blocking and attacking neck temple and ribs. Also referred to as Te Gatana.*

SHUTO JODAN UCHI – Knife–hand high level strike, sword–hand high level strike. *As performed in the Kata Heian Yondan. Also referred to as Te Gatana Jodan Uchi.*

SHUTO MAWASHI UCHI – Circular sword–hand strike, roundhouse knife–hand strike. *Also referred to as Te Gatana Mawashi Uchi.*

SHUTO SOTO MAWASHI UCHI – Circular sword–hand strike, roundhouse knife–hand strike. Strike is executed from outside inwards and with the palm of the hand facing upwards. *Also referred to as Te Gatana Soto Mawashi Uchi.*

SHUTO UCIII – Knife–hand strike, sword–hand strike. *Striking with outside edge of hand. As performed in the Kata Heian Yondan. Also referred to as Te Gatana Uchi.*

SHUTO UCHI MAWASHI UCHI – Circular sword–hand strike, roundhouse knife–hand strike. *Strike is executed from inside outwards and with the palm of the hand facing downwards. Can also be executed by bring striking edge directly down on to the target.*

SOETE – Open hand.

TAISHO (TEISHO):
1) – Palm heel. *The palm of the hand when the fingers are drawn back. The base of the palm is used to attack face, nose, chin, jaw and solar plexus. As performed in the Kata Jion. Can also be used as a block. Also referred to as Shotai and Shotei.*
(2) – Leader, captain of the team.

TAISHO UCHI (TEISHO UCHI) – Palm heel strike. *As performed in the Kata Jion.*

TATE NUKITE – Vertical spear hand, vertical piercing hand, standing spear–hand.

TATE SHUTO – Vertical knife–hand, vertical standing sword–hand.

TATE SHUTO OSAE – Vertical knife hand press, used to push your attacker's punching arm further round than in just a block and therefore turning his body further away from you.

TE GATANA – Knife–hand, sword–hand, knife–edge. *Flat hand with thumb and little finger pressing fingers together. Used on blocking and attacking neck temple and ribs. Also referred to as Shuto.*

TE GATANA UCHI – Knife–hand strike, sword–hand strike. *Striking with outside edge of hand. As performed in the Kata Heian Yondan. Also referred to as Shuto Uchi.*

TEISHO (TAISHO):
1) – Palm heel. *The palm of the hand when the fingers are drawn back. The base of the palm is used to attack face, nose, chin, jaw and solar plexus. As performed in the Kata Jion. Can also be used as a block. Also referred to as Shotai and Shotei.*
(2) – Leader, captain of the team.

TEISHO UCHI (TAISHO UCHI) – **Palm heel strike.** ***As performed in the Kata Jion.***

24

UCHI:
(1) – Strike, strikes, striking.
(2) – Inside, inner.
(3) – Inside outward.

WANTO – Sword arm, arm sword.

WASHIDE – Eagle–hand. *The tips of the fingers are brought together to resemble a birds beak. Used to attack the throat and vital points. As performed in the Kata Gojushiho Dai. Formally called Washi Te.*

WASHIDE AGE UCHI – Eagle–hand rising strike. *As performed in the Kata Gojushiho Dai.*

WASHIDE OTOSHI UCHI – Eagle–hand dropping strike. *As performed in the Kata Gojushiho Dai.*

WASHIDE UCHI – Eagle hand strike.

YONDAN NUKITE (YONHAN NUKITE) – **Four finger spear–hand.** *Flat hand with middle and ring fingers bent so that the tips of all four fingers are flush. The tips of the fingers are used to attack the solar plexus, ribs or chest. Alternative to the more common Shihon Nukite.*

5

Elbow Strikes (Empi Uchi)

This section contains terminology relating to a variety of single offensive striking techniques executed with the elbow.

猿臂打ち

AGE EMPI UCHI (TATE HIJI ATE) – Upward/vertical elbow strike, rising elbow strike. *Also referred to as Tate Empi Uchi.*

EMPI:
(1) – Elbow. *Also referred to as Hiji.*
(2) – Also the name of a Kata and sometimes spelt Enpi.

EMPI CHUDAN MAE UCHI – Middle level elbow strike to the front.

EMPI MAE UCHI – Elbow front strike. *As performed in the Kata Heian Godan.*

EMPI UCHI – Elbow strike. *Use mainly as an attack to the chin, chest, solar plexus and ribs. Also referred to as Hiji–Ate, Hiji Atemi, Hiji Uchi and Sokumen Empi.*

EMPI USHIRO ATE – Elbow strike to the rear. *As performed in the Kata Heian Sandan.*

GYAKU MAWASHI EMPI UCHI – Reverse roundhouse elbow strike.

HIJI – Elbow. *Also referred to as Empi.*

HIJI ATE (HIJE ATE) – Elbow strike. *Use mainly as an attack to the chin, chest, solar plexus and ribs. Also referred to as Empi Uchi, Hiji Uchi, Hiji Atemi and Sokumen Empi.*

HIJI ATEMI (HIJE ATEMI) – Elbow Strike. *Use mainly as an attack to the chin, chest, solar plexus and ribs. Also referred to as Empi Uchi, Hiji Ate, Hiji Uchi and Sokumen Empi.*

HIJI UCHI (HIJE UCHI) – Elbow strike. *Use mainly as an attack to the chin, chest, solar plexus and ribs. Also referred to as Empi Uch, Hiji Ate, Hiji Atemi and Sokumen Empi.*

HIJI WAZA (HIJE WAZA) – Elbow techniques.

HINERI YOKO EMPI UCHI – Twisting lateral elbow strike.

28

KO EMPI UCHI – Rear elbow strike. *Also referred to as Ushiro Empi Uchi.*

MAE EMPI UCHI (MAE EMPI) – Forward elbow strike. *As performed in the Kata Heian Yodan. Also referred to as Mae Hiji Ate.*

MAE HIJI ATE – Forward elbow strike. *As performed in the Kata Heian Yodan. Also referred to as Mae Empi Uchi.*

MAE MAWASHI EMPI UCHI – Forward round–house elbow strike. *Also referred to as Mae Mawashi Hiji Ate.*

MAE MAWASHI HIJI ATE – Forward round–house elbow strike. *Also referred to as Mae Mawashi Empi Uchi.*

MAWASHI EMPI UCHI – Roundhouse elbow strike, circular elbow strike. *Also referred to as Mawashi Hiji Ate.*

MAWASHI HIJI ATE – Roundhouse elbow strike, circular elbow strike. *Also referred to as Mawashi Empi Uchi.*

OTOSHI EMPI UCHI – Downward elbow strike, lowered elbow strike. *Strike by dropping the elbow. Also referred to as Otoshi Hiji Ate.*

OTOSHI HIJI ATE – Downward elbow strike, lowered elbow strike. *Strike by dropping the elbow. Also referred to as Otoshi Empi Uchi.*

SAGETA EMPI UCHI – Downward elbow strike, lowered elbow strike. *Also referred to as Otoshi Empi Uchi.*

SOETE MAE EMPI UCHI (SOETE MAE EMPI) – Supporting front elbow strike, hand assisted front elbow strike.

SOKUMEN EMPI UCHI (SOKUMEN EMPI) – Side elbow strike, side combined elbow strike. The opponent is pulled onto the strike. *As performed in the Kata Tekki Shodan.*

29

TATE EMPI UCHI (TATE EMPI) – Upward/vertical elbow strike, rising elbow strike. *Also referred to as Tate Hiji Ate.*

TATE HIJI ATE – Upward/vertical elbow strike, rising elbow strike. *Also referred to as Tate Empi Uchi.*

TATE MAWASHI EMPI UCHI – Vertical elbow strike, vertical roundhouse elbow strike. *Also referred to as Tate Mawashi Hiji Atei.*

TATE MAWASHI HIJI ATE – Vertical elbow strike, vertical roundhouse elbow strike. *Also referred to as Tate Mawashi Empi Uchi.*

USHIRO EMPI UCHI – Back elbow strike. *Striking to the rear with the elbow. As performed in the Kata Heian Sandan (last move, right arm). Also referred to as Ushiro Hiji Ate.*

USHIRO HIJI ATE – Back elbow strike. *Striking to the rear with the elbow. As performed in the Kata Heian Sandan (last move, right arm). Also referred to as Ushiro Empi Uchi.*

USHIRO MAWASHI EMPI UCHI – Back round–house elbow strike. *Also referred to as Ushiro Mawashi Hiji Atei.*

USHIRO MAWASHI HIJI ATE – Back round–house elbow strike. *Also referred to as Ushiro Mawashi Empi Uchi.*

YOKO EMPI UCHI – Side elbow strike. *Also referred to as Yoko Hiji Ate.*

YOKO HIJI ATE – Side elbow strike. *Also referred to as Yoko Empi Uchi.*

YOKO MAWASHI EMPI UCHI – Side round–house elbow strike. *Striking with the elbow to the side. Also referred to as Yoko Mawashi Hiji Ate.*

YOKO MAWASHI HIJI ATE – Side round–house elbow strike. *Striking with the elbow to the side. Also referred to as Yoko Mawashi Empi Uchi.*

ZEN EMPI UCHI – Front elbow strike. *Also referred to as Mae Empi Uchi.*

6

Striking Techniques
(Uchi Waza)

This section contains terminology relating single strikes and other offensive techniques executed with either an open or closed hand.

打
技

ATEMI – Striking. *Particularly the striking of vital points.*

ATEMI WAZA – Body striking techniques, vital point attacking techniques. *These techniques are normally used in conjunction with grappling and throwing techniques.*

ATERU – Strike.

AWASE–UCHI – Combined strike. A general term for all combined strikes.

CHUDAN TEISHO FURI UCHI – Middle level palm heel circular strike. *As performed in the Kata Chinte.*

CHUDAN UCHI – Middle level, chest, mid–section strike.

CHUDAN YOKO UCHI – Middle level, chest, mid–section side strike.

FURIOROSHI UCHI – Downward swinging strike.

GEDAN UCHI KOMI – Lower level strike.

HIRATE – Flat hand, level hand.

HIRATE DE UTSU – Open hand strike. slap.

IPPON NUKITE – One finger spear strike. *A stabbing action using the extended index finger. Used to attack the eyes or solar plexus.*

KAKUTO UCHI – Wrist joint strike. *Also referred to as Ko Uchi.*

KENTSUI UCHI – Hammer fist strike, bottom fist strike. *Also referred to as Tettsui Uchi.*

KIHON FURI UCHI WAZA – Basic swinging strike techniques.

KIHON UCHI WAZA – Basic striking techniques.

KO UCHI – Bent wrist strike, wrist joint strike. *Also referred to as Kakuto Uchi.*

KOTE UCHI – Forearm strike, wrist strike.

KO UCHI – Wrist joint strike. *Also referred to asKakuto Uchi.*

MAWASHI UCHI – Roundhouse strike.

MIZUNAGARE URAKEN GAMAE (MIZUNAGARE URAKEN KAMAE) – Flowing water back fist. *As performed in the Kata Gojushiho.*

NAKADAKA IPPON KEN – Middle finger one knuckle fist. *Striking with the second knuckle of an extended middle finger of the clenched fist. Used to attack vulnerable and vital points.*

OROSHI FURI UCHI – Downward swinging strike.

OROSHI MAE FURI UCHI – Downward front swinging strike, Uraken.

OROSHI MAWASHI FURI UCHI – Downward diagonal swinging Strike.

OROSHI SOTO FURI UCHI – Downward outward swinging strike.

OROSHI UCHI – Downward strike.

OSAE UCHI – Pressing strike.

OSHI ATERU – Strike.

OTOSHI UCHI – Downward strike.

RIKEN (RIKKEN) – Standing fist, back fist. *Seiken turned through 90 degrees striking with the knuckles*

of the index and middle finger used mainly to attack the face and ribs. Can also be used for blocking.

SASHITE – Rising of the hand to either strike, grab or block.

SHUBO UCHI – Stick hand strike.

SOESHO CHUDAN ZUKI – Attached mid–level strike.

SOETE URAZUKI – Supported close punch.

SOKUMEN TETSUI OTOSHI UCHI – Side hammer–fist dropping strike.

SOKUMEN ZUKI – Side punch.

SOTO–FURI–UCHI – Outward swinging Strike.

SURI UKE ZUKI (SURI UKE TSUKI) – Sliding block punch.

TATE – Vertical, Vertical–fist, vertical–hand.

TATE MAWASHI UCHI – Vertical strike, vertical roundhouse strike.

TATE URAKEN UCHI – Vertical back–fist attack.

TETSUI (TETTSUI) – **Iron fist, hammer fist, mace–hand.** *The attack is delivered with the bottom of the fist. Use to attack head, shoulders, elbow joints, ribs. Can also be used as a block. As performed in the Kata Heian Shodan. Also referred to as Kentsui and Shutsui.*

TETSUI OTOSHI UCHI – Hammer fist dropping strike.

TETSUI UCHI (TETTSUI UCHI) – **Bottom fist strike, hammer fist strike.** *Also referred to as Kentsui Uchi.*

TOBI TETSUI UCHI – Jumping hammer fist strike, jumping bottom fist strike. *The normal target area would be the top of the head or the collar bone.*

UCHI – Strike, strikes, striking. Also means 'inside', 'inner' and 'inside outward'.

UCHIATE – Strike.

UCHI KOMI – Striking thrust., strike.

UCHI MAWASHI UCHI – Roundhouse strike from inside outward.

UCHI OTOSHI – Falling strike.

UCHITE – Striking hand.

UCHI WAZA – Striking techniques.

URAKEN – Back fist, back fist strike. *Striking with the top of the fist using a snapping action and making contact with the knuckles of the index finger and middle finger. Can be executed horizontally from the chest, or up and striking downwards, as performed in the Kata Heian Sandan.*

URAKEN UCHI – Back fist strike. *An extremely fast technique although not as powerful as some other hand techniques.*

URAKEN UCHI TATEMAWASHI – Vertical back fist strike *As performed in the Kata Heian Yondan.*

URAKEN UCHI YOKOMAWASHI – Side roundhouse back fist strike.

YOKO FURI UCHI – Sideward swinging strike.

YOKO MAWASHI UCHI – Horizontal strike. *As performed in the Kata Heian Nidan.*

YOKO UCHI – Side strike, strike to side.

ZUKI UCHI (TSUKI UCHI) – Thrusting strike, punching strike. *Arm is used to block while simultaneously punching the opponent.*

7

Kicking Techniques & Foot/Leg Techniques (Keri Waza To Ashi Waza)

This section contains terminology relating to offensive, defensive and other tactical techniques executed with the foot or leg.

蹴技と脚技

AGE ATE – Rising knee strike. *As performed in the Kata Heian Yondan.*

AGE HAISOKU UCHI – Rising instep strike. *Raising the instep into the attacker's groin. Usually combined with a knee strike. As performed in the Kata Nijushiho.*

ASHI ATE – Foot strike, leg strike.

ASHI BARAI (ASHI HARAI) – Foot sweep, leg sweep.

ASHI GATANA – Edge of foot kick. *Also referred to as Sokuto Geri.*

ASHI SABAKI – Foot movement, foot–work.

ASHI WAZA – Leg and foot techniques.

ASHIBO KAKE UKE – Leg hooking block. *The leg is raised to the side and swung in a circle to deflect an opponents side kick to the abdomen.*

ASHIKUBI KAKE UKE – Ankle hooking block. *Normally used to block a front kick. It is similar in motion to Ashibo Kake Uke.*

CHUDAN MAE GERI – Middle level, chest, mid–section front kick.

CHUDAN MIKAZUKI GERI – Middle level, chest, mid–section cresent kick.

DE ASHI BARAI (DEASHI HARAI) – Advancing forward foot sweep.

ENGETSU UKE – Circular foot block.

FUMIKERI (FUMAKIRI) – Downward cutting kick, slicing kick. *Executed by raising the knee and stamping down with edge of the foot. Usually applied to the knee, shin, or instep of an opponent. As performed in the Kata Bassai Dai.*

40

FUMIKOMI (FUMAKOMI) – **Downward stamping kick.** *Executed by raising the knee and stamping down with the heel of the foot. Usually applied to the knee, shin, or instep of an opponent. As performed in the Kata Heian Sandan.*

FUMI WAZA – Stamping techniques.

GEDAN FUMIKERI – Low level cutting kick, Low level slicing kick. *As performed in the Kata Bassai Dai.*

GEDAN KEKOMI – Trust kick to the groin.

GERI (KERI) – **Kick, kicks.**

GERI NUKE – Slipping through the enemy by kicking.

GERI WAZA (KERI WAZA) – **Kicking techniques.**

GERIGAESHI – Return kick, counter kick. *Performed by kicking a second time without dropping the knee.*

GERIHANASHI – Kick release. *Withdrawing of the leg at the same speed as the kick went in. This is to prevent the vulnerability of standing on one leg and being grabbed or tripped.*

GYAKU ASHI – Reverse foot, reverse leg.

GYAKU MAWASHI GERI – Reverse roundhouse kick. *The target is struck with the ball of the foot (Koshi) from inside out. Also referred to as Ura Mawashi Geri.*

GYAKU MIKAZUKI GERI – Reverse crescent kick. *As performed in the Kata Empi. Also referred to as Ura Mikazuki Geri.*

HAKU GERI – Inward crescent kick. *The striking surface is usually the instep to pad of the foot. This is a Wado Ryu Term.*

41

HARAI FUMIKOMI GERI (BARAI FUMAKOMI KERI) – Sweeping stamping kick. *As performed in the Kata Bassai Dai.*

HAISOKU (HEISOKU) – Instep of the foot. *Used in Keagi to attack the groin and can also be used for Mawashi Geri (roundhouse kick).*

HASAMI GERI – Scissor kick.

HITTSUI GERI – Knee kick. *Mainly used in close range to attack the face, solar plexus, groin and side of the body. Also referred to as Hizagashira and Shittsui.*

HIZA AGE ATE – Rising knee strike. *As performed in the Kata Heian Yondan.*

HIZA ATE – Knee strike. *As performed in the Kata Heian Yondan.*

HIZAGASHIRA – Knee, knee cap. *Used for Hiza Geri at close range to attack the face, solar plexus, groin and side of the body. Also referred to as Shittsui and Hittsui Geri.*

HIZA GERI – Knee kick. As performed in the Kata Empi. Also referred to as Hizken Geri.

HIZATSUI – Knee hammer.

HIZA UCHI – Knee strike. As performed in the Kata Heian Yondan.

HIZA UKE – A blocking action using the knee.

HIZA WAZA – Knee techniques.

HIZA ZUKI (HIZA TSUKI) – Knee strike. *Attack to the groin or to the head by forcing the opponent head down on to the rising knee. As performed in the Kata Heian Yondan.*

JODAN KEKOMI – Upper, high level thrust kick.

JOHO KAITEN TOBI – Jumping turning kick.

JOSOKUTREI – Raised sole. *Used in front and round–house kicks mainly to attack the face, jaw, solar plexus, groin and ribs. Also referred to as Koshi.*

KAKATO – Heel of the foot. *Used in Ushiro Geri (back kick) and Fumikomi (stamping kick) mainly to attack jaw, solar plexus, groin and instep.*

KAKATO GERI – Heel kick, axe kick, stomp kick. *Executed by swinging the straight leg up above the opponents head and striking down with the heel (Kakato).*

KAKE GERI – Hook kick.

KANSETSU GERI – Joint kick, kick against a joint. *Often used against the knee.*

KASEI GERI – Under kick. *Kicking technique executed from under the opponent. As performed in Kata Unsu.*

KEAGE – Kick Up. *Used to describe snapping action as opposed to a thrust. Orginally referred to as Keriage.*

KEBANASHI – Kick off. *Snapping action used to kick the opponent off the leg being held.*

KEKOMI – Thrust. *Term used to describe a thrusting movement of a kick. This term is generally use as a shortened term to describe Yoko Geri Kekomi where the knee is momentarily locked before retracting.*

KERI (GERI) – Kick.

KERIAGE – Kick up. *This is the original name for the term Keage.*

KERIKOME – Kick in. *This is the original name for the term Kekomi. Generally referred to as Keriage.*

KERI NUKE – Slipping through the enemy by kicking.

KERI WAZA (KERI WAZA) – Kicking techniques.

KERU – Kick. *This is used when saying kick as a verb.*

KESA GERI – Diagonal kick.

KIN GERI – Front arch kick, groin kick. *This is not permitted in completion and is considered a foul (Hansoku).*

KINTEKI KOGEKI – Groin kick. *This is not permitted in completion and is considered a foul (Hansoku).*

KIZAMI GERI – Cutting kick, jabbing kick. *Front kick off the front leg, executed with a jabbing action. Also referred to as Kizami Mae Geri.*

KOSHI – Ball of the foot. *Used in Mae Geri (front kick) and Mawashi Geri (roundhouse kick) mainly to attack the face, jaw, solar plexus, groin and ribs. Also referred to as Josokutei. Also means 'hip', 'waist', 'side'.*

MAE ASHI GERI – Front leg kick. *Kicking with the front leg.*

MAE GERI – Front Kick. *Executed by raising knee to in front of the body and the foot is snapped out at the target. The hips are pushed forward for more power and to help gain distance. The foot returns to the knee raised position before retuning to stance.*

MAE GERI KEAGE – Front Snap Kick. *The Knee is raised in front of the body and the foot is snapped out and immediately snapped back to the knee raised position before returning to stance. Also referred to as Mae Keage.*

MAE GERI KEKOMI – Front Thrust Kick. *The Knee is raised in front of the body and the foot is snapped out, the knee is momentarily locked before snapping the*

foot back to the knee raised position and returning to stance. Also referred to as Mae Kekomi.

MAE HAKU GERI – Outward crescent kick. *The striking surface is ashi sokuto. This is a Wado Ryu Term.*

MAE KAKATO GERI – Front heel kick.

MAE KEAGE – Front snap kick.

MAE TOBI GERI – Front jump kick, flying front kick. *Usually executed with kekome (thrust). Also called Nidan Geri.*

MAWASHI GERI (MAEWASHI GERI) – Roundhouse kick. *The knee is raised to the side of the body and then brought sharply round to the front of the body to point at the target causing the foot to snap out to the target. The body leans over to help the hips reach the correct position. The foot is immediately retracted (knee point at target) and the leg is lowered to take up stance (leading leg).*

MAWASHI HIZA GERI – Roundhouse knee kick. *Executed with the same action as a roundhouse kick but striking with the knee.*

MAWASHI TOBI GERI – Roundhouse jumping kick, flying roundhouse kick.

MIKAZUKI GERI (MEKASUKI) – Crescent moon kick, crescent kick, hook kick, drop kick. *Mikazuki means new moon. The kick is use to block an attack by bringing the leg in a hooking movement from outside inwards. As performed in the Kata Heian Godan (the kick strikes the opposite hand).*

MIKAZUKI GERI BARAI – Crescent moon kick block.

MIKAZUKI GERI FUMIKOMI – Stamping crescent kick. *As performed in the Kata Heian Sandan.*

MIKAZUKI GERI UKE – Crescent kick block. *The kick is used to block an attack.*

MOROASHI BARAI – Two leg sweep.

NAMI ASHI – Returning wave, inside leg block.. *Foot technique to block an attack to the groin area. The technique can also be used to strike the opponent's inner thigh or knee. As performed in the Kata Tekki Shodan. Also referred to as Nami Geashi or Nami Ashi Geri.*

NAMI ASHI GERI (NAMI ASHI) – Returning wave, inside leg block.. *Foot technique to block an attack to the groin area. The technique can also be used to strike the opponent's inner thigh or knee. As performed in the Kata Tekki Shodan. Also referred to as Nami Geashi.*

NAMI GAESHI – Returning wave, inside leg block.. *Foot technique to block an attack to the groin area. The technique can also be used to strike the opponent's inner thigh or knee. As performed in the Kata Tekki Shodan. Also referred to as Nami Ashi or Nami Ashi Geri.*

NIDAN GERI – Two level kick, double kick.

NIDAN TOBI GERI – Double jump kick. *One jump with two separate kicks. As performed in the Kata Kanku Dai.*

OKURI ASHI BARAI – Foot sweep, moving on to foot sweep. *The attacker's foot is swept away as he moves forward.*

OSHIKOMI GERI – Pressing–in kick.

REN GERI – Consecutive kicking, double stepping kick.

RENZOKU GERI – Combination kick. *Also referred to as Renraku Geri.*

SANKAKU TOBI – Triangular jump. *As performed in the Kata Meikyo.*

SHITTSUI – Hammer knee. Mainly used in close range to attack the face, solar plexus, groin and side of the body. Also referred to as Hizagashira and Hittsui Geri.

SOKUBO KAKE UKE – Hooking foot block.

SOKUTEI OSAE UKE – Pressing block with sole. *Executed by driving the sole of the foot into to the opponents ankle as he attempts to kick.*

SOKUTEI MAWASHIN UKE – Circular sole block.

SOKUTO – Knife foot, edge of foot. *Used in Yoko Geri Keage (side snap kick) and Yoko Geri Kekomi (side thrust kick). Used with side kicks and stamping mainly to attack jaw, arm–pit, solar plexus and knee.*

SOKUTO GERI – Edge of foot kick. *Also referred to as Ashi Gatana.*

SOKUTO KAKE UKE – Hooking foot block. *Using the edge of the foot.*

SOKUTO KEAGE – Snap kick with edge of foot.

SOKUTO OSAE UKE – Pressing block with edge of foot. *Executed by driving the edge of the foot into to the opponents ankle as he attempts to kick.*

SUNI GERI – Shin kick.

TEISOKU – Sole of the foot. *Used in blocking and crescent kicks mainly to attack the solar plexus.*

TOBIAGARI – Jump.

TOBI ASHI BARAI – Jumping foot sweep. *Used to clear the target area for Tobi Ushiro Geri. As performed in the Kata Kanku Sho.*

TOBI GERI – Jumping kick, jump kick.

47

TOBIKOMI – Jumping.

TOBI USHIRO GERI – Jumping back kick.

TOBI YOKO GERI – Jumping side kick.

TSUGI ASHI – Flowing foot. *Method of moving forward without passing one foot over the other.*

TSUMASAKI – Tips of the toes. Toe kept tightly together and used for kick to the stomach.

TSUMASAKI GERI – Kicking, striking with the tips of the toes. *Used to attack the soft parts of the opponents body e.g. groin.*

UCHI ASHI BARAI – Leg sweep inside outwards.

UCHI MAWASHI GERI – Inside roundhouse kick.

USHIRO ASHI BARAI – Rear leg sweep. *Sweeping an opponent's back leg.*

USHIRO ASHI GERI – Rear leg kick.

USHIRO GERI – Back kick. *Executed by pivoting the body round on the ball of the leading foot to face away from the opponent, ball of kicking foot rests lightly on the ground slightly in front, then the heel is thrust under, straight up and back to strike the target with the heel (Kakato).*

USHIRO GERI KEAGE – Back snap kick.

USHIRO GERI KEKOMI – Back trust kick.

USHIRI KAKATO BARAI – Back heel sweep.

USHIRO KAKATO GERI – Back heel kick.

USHIRO MAWASHI GERI – Reverse round–house kick, back round kick. *The target is struck using the heel (Kakato).*

48

YOKO GERI – Side kick. The knee is raided in front of the body and the body is rotated sideways on to target so that the kick is executed sideways.

YOKO GERI KEAGE – **Side snap kick.** *The knee is raised in front of the body in the direction of the kick, the body is rotated sideways and the foot is snapped out at the target and immediately snapped back, striking with either the edge of the foot (Sokuto) or the instep (Heisoku). Also referred to as Yoko Keage.*

YOKO GERI KEKOMI – **Side thrust kick.** *The knee is raised in front of the body and the body is rotated sideways and the foot is thrust out at the target, knee is momentarily locked straight before snapping the foot back, striking with either the edge of the foot (Sokuto). Also referred to as Yoko Kekomi and occasionally shortened to Kekomi.*

YOKO GERI SOKUTO – Side piercing kick. *Striking with the edge or blade of the foot.*

YOKO SASHI ASHI – Side balance leg.

YOKO TOBI GERI – Side jumping kick, flying side kick.

YORI ASHI – Sliding foot. *Sliding of both feet at the same time without changing stance or posture of the upper body.*

49

8

Blocking Techniques
(Uke Waza)

This section contains terminology relating to single defensive blocking and other tactical techniques executed with the hand, arm or forearm.

受
技

AGE UKE – Rising Block, upper block. *Defense against a Jodan attack. Executed by bringing the blocking arm from the hip, upwards to a point just above the forehead and twisting the forearm so that the back of the fist is pointing towards you.*

AGE UKE GYAKU TSUKAMI – Reverse rising block plus grabbing technique. *Upper body block   and seizing the opponent's weapon, arm, or leg.*

BOGYO ROKU KYODO – Six Defence Actions. *A basic drill of the Japan Karate Do Ryobu–Kai. Uses the old names of the six techniques Age Te, Harai Te (or Gedan Barai), Soto Yoko Te, Uchi Yoko Te, Shuto Te and Sukui Te.*

BARAI – Sweep.

BARAI UKE – Sweeping block.

CHUDAN BARAI – Middle level, chest, mid–section block.

CHUDAN BARAI UKE – Middle level, chest, mid–section sweeping block.

CHUDAN HAISHU UKE – Middle level, chest, mid–section backhand block. *As performed in the Kata Heian Godan.*

CHUDAN KAKE UKE – Middle level, chest, mid–section hooking block.

CHUDAN KAKIWAKE UKE – Middle level, chest, mid–section wedge block. *As performed in the Kata Heian Yondan.*

CHUDAN SOTO UKE – Middle level chest mid–section bock, outside inwards.

CHUDAN SHUTO UKE – Middle level, chest, mid–section knife hand block.

CHUDAN UCHI UDE UKE – Middle level, chest, mid–section inside forearm block.

52

CHUDAN UCHI UKE – Middle level, chest, mid–section inside block.

CHUDAN UDE UKE – Middle level, chest, mid–section forearm block.

CHUDAN UKE – Middle level, chest, mid–section block.

EMPI SURI UKE – Elbow sliding block. *This is a combination block and punch. The arm is bent for the block and then straightened in a snapping motion to deliver the punch. As performed in the Kata Heian Nedan. Also referred to as Hiji Suri Uke.*

EMPI UKE – Elbow block. *A general term for the blocking action using the elbow. Also referred to as Hiji Uke.*

FUMIKOMI AGE UKE – Upper rising block, stepping in.

FUMIKOMI SHUTO UKE – Outside forearm block, stepping in.

GASSHO UKE – Block with palm heels together. *As performed in the Kata Hangetsu.*

GEDAN BARAI (GEDAN BARAI UKE) – Lower level sweep, downward block. *Used to guard against an attack to the groin or lower body. Executed by bringing the fist of the blocking arm from the top of the opposite shoulder to a point approximately 15cm above the knee. As performed in the Kata Heian Shodan.*

GEDAN KAKE UKE – Lower level hooking block, Downward hooking block. *Either executed from the outside inwards to deflect a kick with the back of the hand or from inside outwards using the opposite arm to the leading leg sweeping across the body and hooking the opponent's ankle. As performed in Bassai Dai.*

53

GEDAN SHUTO UKE – Lower level knife hand block. *As performed in the Kata Heian Godan.*

GEDAN SOTO UDE UKE – Lower level outside forearm block. *As performed in the Kata Tekki Nidan.*

GEDAN SUKUI UKE – Low level scooping block, lower level hooking block. *As performed in the Kata Bassai Dai.*

GEDAN UCHI BARAI – Low level sweeping block.

GEDAN UCHI UKE – *Lower level block from the inside outwards.*

GEDAN UDE UKE – Low level forearm block.

GEDAN UKE – Downward block, lower level block.

GYAKU AGE UKE – Reverse Upper rising block, reverse upward block. *Used to guard against an attack to the face or head. Executed with the blocking arm on the opposite side to the leading leg.*

GYAKU GEDAN BARAI – Reverse lower level sweep, reverse downward block. *Used to guard against an attack to the groin or lower body. Executed with the blocking arm on the opposite side to the leading leg.*

GYAKU UCHI UKE – Reverse forearm block, reverse striking block.
Executed with the blocking arm on the opposite side to the leading leg.

GYAKU UDE UKE – Reverse forearm block. *Executed with the blocking arm on the opposite side to the leading leg.*

HAISHU AWASE UKE (HAISHO AWASE UKE) – Back–hand combined block. *As performed in the Kata Gankaku.*

HAISHU JUJI UKE (HAISHO JUJI UKE) – Back–hand crossed block.

HAISHU UKE (HAISHO UKE) – Back–hand block. *A block using the back of the hand. As performed in the Kata Heian Godan.*

HAITO GEDAN BARAI – Ridge–hand downward sweep. *As performed in the Kata Heian Nidan.*

HAITO UKE – Ridge–hand block.

HAIWAN NAGASHI UKE – Back arm sweeping block.

HAIWAN UKE – Back arm block. *As performed in the Kata Heian Nidan (first move, left arm).*

HARAI TE – Sweeping hand block. *This technique clears space for a counter.*

HIJI BARAI – Elbow sweeping block.

HIJI UKE – Elbow block. *A general term for the blocking action using the elbow. Also referred to as Empi Uke.*

HINERI UKE – Twisting block, twisting hand block.

HIRATE OSAE UKE – Forehand pressing block. *As performed in the Kata Kanku Sho.*

JODAN AGE UKE – Upper, high level block. Used to defend against a head attack.

JODAN MOROTE UKE – Upper level augmented forearm block. *As performed in the Kata Jion.*

JODAN NAGASHI UKE – Upper, high level sweeping block.

JODAN SHUTO UKE – Upper, high level knife–hand block.

JODAN SOTO YOKO TE – Upper, high level outside side–hand block. *Also referred to as Jodan Uchi Uke.*

JODAN TSUKAMI UKE – Upper, high level grasping block.

55

JODAN UCHI UKE – Upper, high level forearm block from the inside outwards. *Also referred to as Jodan Soto Yoko Te.*

JODAN UKE – Upper, high level block.

JODAN YOKO UCHI BARAI – Upper, high level side sweeping block.

JODAN YOKO UKE – Upper, high level side block.

JO UKE – Jo block.

JO UKE WAZA – Jo blocking techniques.

KAISHO UKE (KAISHU UKE) – Open hand block.

KAKAE UKE – Circular, pulling block. *The block emphasizes the uses of shote, or heel of the hand.*

KAKAE TE UKE – Trapping hand block.

KAKE SHUTO UKE (KAGI SHUTO UKE) – Hooking knife hand block. *Similar to Tate Shuto Uke but the body swings further around to the back.*

KAKE TE (KAGI TE) – Hook block. *As performed in the Kata Tekki Shodan.*

KAKE TE UKE (KAGI TE UKE) – Trapping hand block.

KAKE UKE (KAGI UKE) – Hooking block.

KAKUTO UKE – Bent wrist block, wrist joint block. *Also known as Ko Uke.*

KAISHU UKE (KAISHO UKE) – Open hand block.

KAISHU HAIWAN UKE (KAISHO HAIWAN UKE) – Open–hand back arm block. *As performed in the Kata Heian Yondan (first move, left arm).*

56

KASUI UKE – Fire and water block. As performed in the Kata Kanku Sho.

KATATE UKE – One/single hand block.

KEITO UKE – Chicken head wrist block. *An upward block that make full us of the snapping wrist.*

KEITO UKE NAGASHI – Chicken head wrist blocking sweep. *As performed in the Kata Gojushiho Dai.*

KENTSUI UKE – Hammer fist block. *Also referred to as Tettsui Uke.*

KIHON FURI UKE WAZA – Basic swinging block techniques.

KIHON UKE WAZA – Basic blocking techniques.

KOKO UKE – Tiger mouth block.

KO UKE – Crane block, arch block. *Same as Kakuto–Uke.*

MAEUDE DEAI OSAE UKE – Forearm pressing block.

MAEUDE HINDERI UKE – Forearm twisting block.

NAGASHI UKE (NAGASHI) – Sweeping block, flowing block. Generally an open hand is used to redirect the attack. As performed in the Kata Heian Nidan (second move, left arm).

OROSHI FURI UKE – Downward swinging block.

OROSHI MAWASHI FURI UKE – Downward diagonal swinging Block.

OROSHI SOTO FURI UKE – Downward outward swinging block.

OROSHI UKE – Downward block.

OSAE UKE – Pressing block, forearm pressing block. *As performed in the Kata Heian Sandan.*

OSHI UKE – Pushing block.

OTOSHI UKE – Dropping block. *Arm is bent at a 90° angle as in Ude Uke but drops down from above your head to strike opponents forearm.*

SAGI ASHI OROSHI FURI UKE – Downward swinging block in crane stance.

SEIRYUTO UKE – Ox jaw block, bull jaw block. *A hand technique delivered with the base of the Shuto (knife–hand) as a block.*

SHITA UKE – Downward block.

SHO SUKUI UKE (**SUKUI UKE**) – Scooping palm block, Scooping Block. *Executed by blocking from outside and catching the knee in the other hand.*

SHUTO GEDAN BARAI – Knife–hand downward sweep, sword–hand low level sweep. *As performed in the Kata Heian Yondan.*

SHUTO TE – Knife–hand bock, sword–hand block. *Also referred to as Shuto Uke.*

SHUTO UKE – *Executed by bringing the open blocking hand from the top of the opposite shoulder to a terminal position as in Ude Uke but with palm of the open hand facing front. Non–blocking hand draws back to solar| plexus with palm facing up. To defend against a Chudan attack as performed in the Kata Heian Shodan.*

SOKUMEN TATE SHUTO UKE – Side vertical knife–hand block.

SOKUMEN UKE – Side block.

SOTO–FURI–UKE – Outward swinging block.

SOTO MAWASHI UCHI – Roundhouse strike form outside inward.

SOTO MAWASHI UKE – Roundhouse block form outside inward.

SOTO UDE UKE – Outer forearm block, forearm block from outside inwards. *Executed by raising blocking arm to the side of the head with elbow bent at a 90° angle and bringing it in a wide arc across the body, from outside, inside ,twisting the forearm on contact so back of fist ends facing forward and top of fist is level with the shoulder. To defend against Chudan attack as performed in the Kata Bassai Dai. Also referred to as Uchi Yoko Te.*

SOTO UKE – Outside middle block. *Block from outside using the bottom of wrist.*

SOTO YOKO TE – Outside side–hand block.

SUKUI TE – Scooping block. *Also referred to as Sukui Uke.*

SUKUI UKE – Scooping block. *Executed from the outside inwards to deflect a kick with the back of the open hand or from inside outwards using the opposite arm to the leading leg sweeping across the body and hooking the opponents' ankle with an open hand or fist.*

SURI UKE ZUKI (SURI UKE TSUKI) – Sliding block punch.

TATE SHUTO UKE – Vertical knife–hand block, upward sword–hand block. *Executed with a straight elbow and bent but firm wrist. As performed in the Kata Heian Sandan.*

TAE UKE – Position of the arms where one arm is across the chest, palm down and parallel to the ground and the other arm is pulled back beside the chest palm up.

TE GATANA UKE – Hand–sword block.

TE OSAE UKE – Hand pressing block. *As performed in the Kata Heian Sandan.*

TEISHO AWASE UKE – Combined palm heel block.

TEISHO BARAI – Palm heel sweep. *As performed in the Kata Unsu.*

TEISHO UKE – Palm–heel block. *Executed by bringing arm in with wrist bent inward and snapping wrist forward at impact, striking with heel of hand to opponent's wrist. As performed in the Kata Empi.*

TEKUBI AWAZI UKE – Rolling wrist lock.

TEKUBI KAKE UKE – Wrist hooking block, wrist hook block. *The hook is formed by bending the hand backwards at the wrist as performed in the Kata Empi.*

TE NAGASHI UKE – Hand sweeping block. *Executed by deflecting the punch with palm of open hand past your head, twisting the hand on impacts so that the palm faces your ear. As performed in the Kata Heian Godan.*

TENCHI UKE – Heaven and earth block. Simultaneously perform the same blocking technique, one high and one low.

TE OSAE UKE – Hand pressing block.

TETTSUI UKE (TETSUI UKE) – Hammer fist block, bottom fist block. *Also referred to as Kentsui Uke.*

TSUKAMI UKE – Grasping block. As performed in the Kata Bassai Dai.

TSUKI UKE (ZUKI UKE) – Striking block, thrusting block, punching block.

UCHI TE – Striking block. *Can be use to either defend or attack.*

UCHI UDE UKE – Inside forearm block, striking arm block, Inner forearm block, blocking from inside outwards. *The block is executed by bringing the fist of the blocking arm across the body from under the non-blocking arm, from inside outside, to defend against a Chudan attack.*

UCHI UKE – Forearm block, striking block, inside outward block.

UCHI YOKO TE – Outside forearm block. *The block is executed in a wide arc to defend against a Chudan attack. As performed in the Kata Bassai Dai. Also referred to as Soto Ude Uke.*

UDE – Forearm, arm. *Mainly used for blocking, particularly the outer, inner and upper areas adjacent to the wrist. Also referred to as Shubo and Wanto.*

UDE SOETE – Forearm block. *As performed in the Kata Heian Nidan (first move with right arm).*

UDE UKE – Forearm block.

UKE – Block, defender. *The strict translation is more in keeping with receiving and catching an attack.*

UKE GAE – Changing blocks.

UKE KIME – Blocking and finishing.

UKE KIME ICHIJO – Blocking and finishing with one technique.

UKE WAZA – Blocking techniques.

UKE TE – Hand blocks, hand defence, blocking hand.

61

UKE ZUKI – block punch.

URAKEN UKE – Back fist block.

USHIRO GEDAN BARAI – **Backward lower level sweep.**
As performed in the Kata Empi.

WA UKE – Circle block. *The path taken is a half–circle and at the end of the block the hand is angled slightly to the outside.*

WASHIDE UKE – Eagle–hand block.

YOKO BARAI – Side block.

YOKO UKE – Side block, sideward block.

ZUKI UKE (TSUKI UKE) – Thrusting block, punching block.

9

Two Handed Blocks
(Morote Uke Waza)

This section contains terminology relating two handed defensive blocking and other tactical techniques executed with the hand, arm or forearm.

諸手受け技

AWASE AGE UKE – Combined upper rising block. *Both arms are raised together performing the block to defend against an attack to the upper body. As performed in the Kata Bassai Dai.*

AWASE KOKO UKE – Combined tiger mouth block. *Defence against a Jo or Bo attack. As performed in the Kata Empi.*

AWASE MAWASHI KAKE UKE – Combined round house hooking block. *Can used to unbalance or throw the attacker. As performed in the Kata Nijushiho.*

AWASE MAWASHI UKE – Combined roundhouse block. *As performed in the Kata Kankau Dai.*

AWASE SHUTO AGE UKE – Combined knife hand rising block. *The thumbs touch forming a triangle. As performed in the Kata Chinte.*

AWASE UKE – Combination blocks.

GEDAN JUJI UKE – Downwards X–block, lower level cross block. *A double handed block used as a defence against a front kick. Wrists are crossed at low level to catch or restrain an attacking kick. As performed in the Kata Heian Yondan.*

HAISHU–AWASE–UKE – Backhand combined block. *As performed in the Kata Gankaku (first move).*

HASAMI UKE – Scissors block. *As performed in the Kata Nijushiho and Wankan.*

JODAN JUJI UKE – Upper, high level cross X block. *As performed in the Kata Jion.*

JODAN KAKIWAKE UKE – Upper, high level reverse wedge block.

JODAN KOSA UKE – Upper, high level cross block.

JODAN MOROTE UKE – Upper level two–handed block, Upper level augemented block. *As performed in the KatavJion.*

JUJI UKE – Crossed X block. *Wrists are crossed to catch or deflect an attacking kick, punch or strike. As performed in the Kata Heian Godan.*

KAKIWAKE UKE – Wedging block, reverse wedging block. *Two handed block used as a defence against a grab to the chest area or throat. Executed by pushing both hands with wrists crossed forwards between his arms and your face, then force forearms down and outwards twisting your wrists down to break his grip. As performed in the Kata Heian Yondan.*

KAISHU KOSA UKE (KAISHO KOSA UKE) – Open hand cross block. *As performed in the Kata Hangetsu and Gojushiho.*

KOSA UKE – Crossed block. *As performed in the Kata Heian Sandan (second and third move).*

MANJI UKE – A Double block. *Passing high and low block. One arm executes Gedan Barai in front of the body, while the other arm executes Jodan Uchi Uke as performed in the Kata Jion or Jodan Soto Yoko Te to the rear as performed in the Kata Heian Godan.*

MOROTE AGE UKE – Double handed upper level block. *As performed in the Kata Bassai Dai.*

MOROTE GEDAN UKE – Double handed lower level block. *As performed in the Kata Gankaku.*

MOROTE JODAN UCHI UKE – Upper, high level block inside outwards with both hands.

MOROTE JODAN UKE – Double handed upper level block.

MOROTE JO UKE – Double handed Jo block.

MOROTE KAISHU GEDAN UKE – Double open handed lower level block. *As performed in the Kata Gojushiho.*

MOROTE KOKO DORI – Double handed tiger mouth grab/catch. *As performed in the Kata Jitte.*

MOROTE KOKO UKE – Double tiger mouth block.

MOROTE KUBI OSAE – Double handed neck press, double handed neck hold. *As performed in the Kata Heian Yondan.*

MORATE KUBI OSAE – Double handed neck press. *As performed in the Kata Heian Yondan.*

MOROTE SUKUI UKE – Double handed scooping block.

MOROTE TSUAKMI UKE – Double handed grasping block.

MOROTE UDE UKE (MOROTE UKE) – **Augmented forearm block, double handed block.** *One arm and fist is used to support the other arm in a block. Similar to Uchi Uke but with the fist of the non–blocking arm bracing the forearm of the blocking arm. As performed in the Kata Heian Nidan.*

MUSO UKE – Vertical scissors forearm block. *As performed in the Kata Sochin.*

NAIWAN KAKIWAKE – Forearm wedging block.

ROWAN GAMAE –Double downwards block. *As performed in the Kata Jion.*

RYO SHO SOKUMEN – Side block with both hands.

RYO SHO TSUKAMI UKE – Two–handed grasping block.

RYO UDE MAEWASHI UKE – Wide forearm roundhouse block. *As performed in the Kata Kanku Dai.*

RYOWAN UCHI UKE – Both arm striking block, double forearm inside block. *As performed in the Kata Jion. Also know as Sowan Uchi Uke.*

RYU UDE MAWASHI UKE – Double round forearm block. *As performed in the Kata Kanku Dai.*

RYU UN NO UKE – *Double hand supporting block. As performed in the Kata Gojushiho.*

RYU WAN GEDAN KAKIWAKI UKE – Double arm lower level wedge block. *As performed in the Kata Jion and Jitte.*

SHUTO JUJI UKE – **Knife–hand cross block, sword–hand cross block.** *As performed in the Kata Heian Godan.*

SHUTO KAKIWAKI – Knife–hand wedging, sword–hand wedging. *The same movement as Kakiwake Uke but the hands are open and the palms directed away from the body.*

SOETE SOKUMEN UKE – Hand assisted side block, supported forearm side block. *As performed in the Kata Tekki Nidan.*

SOKUMEN AWASE UKE (SOKUMEN AWASE) – Side combined block, side two–hand block. *Hands are positioned back to back, fingers pointing upwards and palms used to deflect an attack to the side of the head. As performed in the Kata Gankaku.*

SOKUMEN SOETE GEDAN UCHI UDE UKE – Side–hand assisted lower level inside forearm block.

SOWAN UCHI UKE – Both arm striking block, double forearm inside block. *As performed in the Kata Jion. Also know as Ryowan Uchi Uke.*

SOWAN UKE – Both arm block.

TEISHO AWASE UKE – Combined Palm Heel–Block. *Place heel of hands together and bend hands back, push forward and down to opponent's leg. As performed in the Kata Hangetsu.*

TEISHO AWASE GEDAN UKE – Palm heel combined low level block. *Heels of both palms are placed together, hands bent back and pushed forwards and down the opponents' leg. As performed in the Kata Hangetsu.*

TEISHO KOSA UKE – Palm heel crossed block.

TEISHO MOROTE UKE – Palm heel two handed block.

YAMA KAKIWAKE – Mountain wide U wedging block. *As performed in the Kata Jitte.*

YAMA UKE – Mountain/wide U block. *A wide U shaped dual block.*

YOKO UDE HASAMI UKE – Side forearm scissors block. *An advanced block as performed in the Kata Tekki Sandan.*

10

Other Defensive Techniques (Sonohoka No Bougyo Waza)

This section contains terminology relating a variety of grabs, pressing blocks, sweeps, locks and other defensive techniques.

その他の防御技

ASHIBO KAKE UKE – Leg hooking block. *Leg is lifted to the side and swung across to the body in an arc to catch the back of ankle of the opponents Kekome with the shin.*

ASHI HISHIGI – Leg lock, leg crunch. *Pressure is applied to opponent's lower calf in order to pin him to the floor.*

AWASE HIKI TSUKAMI – Combined pulling grasp. As performed in the Kata Heian Godan.

ASHI KUBI KAKE UKE (ASHI KUBE KAKE UKE) – Ankle hooking block. *The ankle is hooked up below the calf of the opponents Mae Geri.*

ASHI KUBI WAZA – Ankle locking techniques.

BARAI (HARAI) – Sweep.

BARAI TE (HARAI TE) – Sweeping technique with the arm.

BARAI WAZA (HARAI WAZA) – Sweeping techniques.

CHUDAN OSAE UKE – Middle level, chest, mid–section pressing block.

CHUDAN OSHI AGE UKE – Middle level, chest, mid–section upward pressing block.

DEAL OSAE – Suppressing attack.

DEAL OSAE UKE – Pressing block stepping in. *Encountering as the attack comes forward and suppressing it with a press block.*

DORI – Grab, pull, hold.

ENGETSU UKE – Circle foot block.

ERI SEOI NAGE – Lapel shoulder throw.

ERI TSUKAMI – Lapel grab.

FURI KOSA BARAI – Circular cross sweep. *As performed in the Kata Nijushiho.*

FUSE – Defence, ground.

GATAME – Locking, holding, arm lock.

GEDAN OSAE UKE – Low level pressing block.

GEDAN SHUTO OSAE – Lower level knife hand press. *As performed in the Kata Gojushiho Dai.*

GYAKU KANSETSU – Against the Joint.

GYAKU TE DORI – Reverse hand grab. *As performed in the Kata Gankaku.*

HAITO KAKIWAKE – Ridge–hand wedging.

HAITO SUKUI NAGE – Ridge–hand scooping throw. Used to counter a front kick. The attacker's kicking leg is scooped up high to take him off balance.

HAZUSHI – Pulling away.

HARAI (BARAI) – Sweep.

HARAI TE (BARAI TE) – Sweeping technique with the arm, sweeping hand.

HARAI WAZA (BARAI WAZA) – Sweeping techniques.

HARAU – Parry.

HASAMI (UDE) UKE HIZA KAMAE – Scissor (forearm) block knee posture. *Both forearms execute a scissor block as the knee is raised to attack the groin.*

HAZUSHI TE – Pulling away hand. *The action of pulling away the hand after is has been grabbed. As performed in the Kata Heian Shodan.*

HIKI – Pulling.

HIKI TE – **Withdrawing hand, pulling in block, both hands retracting.** *Executed by pulling and twisting the attacking arm of an opponent. This technique is used to unbalance the attacker allowing an effective counter moving forward and using for example a strike backward with the elbow.*

HINERI KAESHI – Twist counter. *As performed in the Kata Kanku Sho.*

HIRATE OSAE UKE – Fore–hand pressing block, flat hand pressing block.

HIZA UKE – Knee block. *Blocking action using the knee.*

KAESHI DORI – Attached palm hand catch.

KAGI – Hooking.

KAKAE NAGE – Trapping throw.

KAKE – Hooking.

KAKE–TE – Hooking hand.

KAKE DORI – Hooking catch/grasp/pull. *As performed in the Kata Hangetsu.*

KAKIWAKE (KAKIWAKI) – **Two handed wedging movement.** *This technique is used to break the hold of the opponent. The outer surface of the wrist is used to neutralize a two–handed attack, such as a grab. As performed in the Kata Heian Yondan.*

KAKUTO UCHI – Wrist joint strike. *Also referred to as Ko Uchi.*

KAMI – Hair. *Also referred to as Ke.*

KAMI TSUKAMI – Hair Grab.

KAMITSUKU – Bite.

KAMI ZUKAMI (KAMI TSUKAMI) – Hair grasping. *As performed in the Kata Empi.*

KANSETSU– Against the joint, joint lock. *Locking techniques against joints. Also means 'joint', 'knuckles'.*

KANSETSU UCHI – Joint strike.

KANSETSU WAZA – Locking techniques, against the joint techniques.

KATAME WAZA – Grappling techniques.

KE–TSUKAMI – Hair grab. *Also referred to as Kami Tsukami.*

KOHO OSAE – Rear grab. A bear hug from the rear.

KOKO HIZA KUZUSHI – Tiger mouth knee pull down. *As performed in the Kata Nijushiho.*

KOKO OSAE – Tiger mouth grasp.

KOMANAGE – Spinning top. *Throwing technique executed by placing a hand in the arm pit area of the attacker whilst the other hand holds the wrist and the attacker is forced down.*

KOTE GAESHI – Outside wrist–twist.

KOTE HODOKI WAZA – Wrist releasing techniques.

KOTE JIME – Wrist lock.

KO UCHI – Wrist joint strike. *Also referred to as Kakuto Uchi.*

KUBIWA – Neck circle or "to encircle the neck". *This is a throwing technique where you encircle your opponent's neck* *with your arm and then force his head and body off balance backwards throwing him to the ground.*

KUBOTAN – A key chain used as a self–defence weapon developed by Takayuki Kubota.

MIKAZUKI BARAI – Crescent sweep.

MOROTE KOKO DORI – Double tiger mouth grasp.

MOROTE KUBI OSAE – Two handed head hold, two handed neck hold. *Both hands are used to grab either side of the opponents head. As performed in the Kata Heain Yondan.*

NAGASU – To flow like water. Deflection of an on–coming attack. *This term describes being carried by a current in a stream. So this relates to Nagashi Uke in which you re–direct the attack as it moves closer to you, sweeping is just past you.*

NAGE WAZA – Throwing technique.

NAMI GAESHI – Returning wave. *The sole of the foot is used to deflect a Gedan kick. As performed in the Kata Tekki Shodan.*

NIGIRU – Clasp, hold, hold tight.

OSAE – Pressing, press down.

OSHI – Pushing. *This is not permitted in completion and is considered a foul (Hansoku).*

OSHIKOMU – Push forcefully.

OSHINOBASU – Push, extend.

RYO HIJI HARAI AGE – Both elbows sweeping rising.

SEN – Defensive techniques, power.

SEOI NAGE – Shoulder throw.

SHIME – Strangle, choke.

SHIME WAZA – Strangulation techniques.

SHUTO OSAE – Knife–hand press, sword–hand press. *As performed in the Kata Gojushiho Dai.*

SOEDSHO KAESHI UDE – Palm assisted counter forearm. *Advanced block/release as performed in the Kata Tekki Sandan.*

SOESHO KAESHI UDE – Attached palm hand arm.

SOETE – Hand assisted, supported arm. *One arm is used to support the other.*

SOKUBO KAKE UKE – Hooking foot block.

SOKUTEI MAWASHI UKE – Circular block with sole of the foot.

SOKUTO OSAE UKE – Foot edge pressing block. *Pressing block with the edge of the foot.*

SOKUTEI OSAE UKE – Pressing block with sole of the foot. *Raise the blocking foot and drive the sole into your opponent's ankle as he begins to kick*

SUIHEI BO DORI – Horizontal bo grasp.

SUNDOME – No contact, arresting a technique.

SUNE UKE – Shin block. *Generally used against a roundhouse kick.*

TANIOTOSHI – To push off a cliff. A type of shoulder throw. The defender grasps the attacker's arm and steps in, placing his shoulder under the attacker's arm pit and forcing him down.

TE TSUKAMI – Hand grasp.

TE WAZA – Hand techniques.

TEISHO BARAI – Palm heel sweep.

TSUBAMEGAESHI – V–turning swallow. *A throwing technique.*

TSUKAMI (ZUKAMI) – Grasp, grasping. *Also referred to as Tsukamu.*

TSUKAMI WAZA – Catching technique, grasping technique. *A blocking technique by seizing the opponent's weapon, arm, or leg. Used often for grappling techniques.*

TSUKAMIYOSE – Grasping–pulling, grasp–pull.

TUITE – Grappling skills.

TUITE WAZA – Grappling hand techniques.

USHIRO OSAE KOMI – Rear hold. A bear hug from behind.

UDEWA – To encircle with the arm. *Throwing technique.*

UKEMI – Break–fall, break–falling.

UKEMI WAZA – Break–fall techniques.

YOSE – Pulling.

11

Stances & Posture
(Dachi To Kamae)

This section contains terminology relating stances, postures, positions and other transitional body movements.

立ちと構え

AGE – Rising, upper.

AGURA WO KAKU – Informal seating position.

AI KAMAE (AI GAMAE) – Harmony posture.

ANTACHI WAZA – Position at the beginning of a movement when one of the opponents is standing *(Tachi)* and the other is on there knees *(Suwari).*

ANTEI – Balance.

ASHI FUMIKAE – Changing legs, changing feet.

ASHI NO TACHI KATA – Method of placing the feet on the ground in anticipation of an attack or in preparation for a counter–attack.

AYUMI – Step, pace.

AYUMI ASHI – Stepping foot. *Method of footwork, where the feet move alternatively one ahead of the other each sliding along the floor.*

AYUMI DACHI – Natural walking stance *with the weight over the centre. A stance found in Itosu Kai Shito Ryu.*

CHUDAN KAMAE (CHUDAN GAMAE) – Middle level, mid–section posture.

CHUDAN NO KAMAE (CHUDAN NO GAMAE) – Middle level, chest, mid–section guard. *A freestyle posture where the hands are held at middle level.*

CHUDAN URAKEN KAMAE (CHUDAN URAKEN GAMAE) – Middle level, chest, mid–section back fist posture. *As performed in the Kata Hangetsu.*

DACHI – Stance.

DE – Advancing.

DO – Movement, activity. Also means 'way', 'path of life', 'torso' and 'trunk of the body'.

DO KYAKU – Moving leg.

DOJI – Simultaneous.

FU ANTI – Instability, lack of balance.

FUDO DACHI – Rooted Stance, diagonal straddle leg stance. Rooted or immovable stance. Also referred to as Sochin Dachi. Modified front stance from the Kata Sochin.

FUMIDASHI – The movement into Zenkutsu Dachi, the straightening of the pivot leg strongly, keeping the hips level and lightly but quickly sliding the moving leg forward.

FURI – Swing, circular, round.

FURIAGE – Upward swing, swing up.

FURIKAERU – Turn (look) round, rotate and look back.

FURI (FURISUTE) – Swinging, swing.

FUSE NO SHISEI – Going–to–ground position.

FUSERU – Lie flat.

GAESHI – Twist.

GAMAE (KAMAE):
(1) – **Ready position of the hands.** *A combative posture or stance either with or without a weapon. The stance indicate a mental attitude or frame of mind the process of "switching on".*
(2) – **Kamae may also connote proper distance (Ma–ai) with respect to one's partner.** *Although Kamae generally refers to a physical stance, there is an important parallel in Karate between one's physical and one's psychological bearing. Adopting a strong*

physical stance helps to promote the correlative adoption of a strong psychological attitude. It is important to try so far as possible to maintain a positive and strong mental bearing in Karate.

GANKAKU DACHI – Crane stance. *Also referred to as Tsuru Ashi Dachi and Sagi Ashi Dachi.*

GANKAKU KAMAE (GANKAKU GAMAE) – Crane posture, crane on a rock posture. *The legs are in Tsuru Ashi Dachi and the arms in Manji Uke. As performed in the Kata Gankaku.*

GAWA – Side.

GEDAN KAMAE (GEDAN GAMAE) – Low level posture, downward blocking position. *As performed in the Kata Kanku Dai.*

GYAKU – Reverse, opposite.

GYAKU HANMI – Reverse half–front facing position.

GYAKU HOMINI – Reverse hip twist.

GYAKU KAITEN – Reverse rotation. *Where the rotation of the hips are in the opposite direction as the technique. e.g. Gedan Barai.*

GYAKU NEKO ASHI DACHI – Reverse cat stance. *Feet are roughly in the same position as in Neko Ashi Dachi but the rear heel is up while the front heel is down. The rear knee generally points inward. Weight is more on the front foot.*

GYAKU TE – Reverse hand.

GYAKUZUKI DACHI (GYAKUTSUKI DACHI) – Reverse punch stance. *Front foot is one foot length wider and one foot length shorter than Junzuki Dachi. Front foot points in slightly. Weight is more on the front foot.*

GYAKUZUKI NO TSUKOMI DACHI (GYAKUTSUKI NO TSUKKOMI DACHI) – Back stance, Rearward lunging stance. *A stance which has most of the weight to the back leg. Also referred to as Kokutsu Dachi.*

GYAKUZUKI TSUKOMI DACHI (GYAKUTSUKI TSUKKOMI DACHI) – Reverse lunge punch stance. *Front foot heel is even with rear foot toes on a line perpendicular to the attack line. Both feet point slightly inward. Distance between feet is roughly two and one half shoulder widths. Body leans slightly forward. Weight is more on the front foot.*

HACHIJI DACHI (HACHINOJI DACHI) – Open leg, natural stance. *Feet positioned about one shoulder width apart, with feet pointed slightly outward and arms relaxed with fists clenched and held in front of the body.*

HACHIJI DACHI SHIZEN TAI (HACHINOJI DACHI SHIZEN TAI) – Open leg, natural stance natural position.

HAIMEN – Back or rear side.

HAITO KOSHI KAMAE (HAITO KOSHI GAMAE) – Ridge–hand hip posture. The bottom hand is held as Seiken and the top hand is held in Haito with the palm facing up.

HANGETSU DACHI – Half–moon stance. *Legs shoulder width apart with front foot turned in at 45 degree angle to back foot pointing forwards and with knees turned in to protect the groin. As performed in the Kata Hangetsu.*

HANMI – Half–front facing position.

HANMI KAMAE (HANMI GAMAE) – Half facing posture, fighting stance, freestyle posture.

HANMI SASHI ASHI – Half–facing balance leg. *As performed in the Kata Hangetsu.*

HANMI SASHI ASHI DACHI – Half front facing stepping across stance. *As performed in the Kata Hungestsu.*

HANMI KAESHI DORI – Half–facing counter.

HAN ZENKUTSU DACHI – Half front stance. *The feet are half the full stance distance apart.*

HEIKO – Parallel.

HEIKO DACHI – Parallel stance, natural stance. *Feet positioned about one shoulder width apart, feet pointed straight forward and with arms relaxed and with fists clenched. Some Kata begin from this position.*

HEIKO DACHI *(Higaonna Line)* – A heiko dachi stance but the front foot is turned slightly inwards and the rear foot is straight.

HEISOKU DACHI – Informal Attention Stance. *Feet together, heels and toes together and pointed straight forward, arms relaxed with fists clenched and held at the side and away from the body.*

HENKA WAZA – Changing techniques.

HENTE – Changing hands. The action of blocking and then immediately punching with the same hand or punching and then immediately blocking with the same hand.

HENTE WAZA – Changing hands techniques.

HIDARI (HADARI) – Left, left–hand side. *Usually used in connection with stances.*

HIDARI ASHI DACHI – Left leg stance.

HIDARI KAMAE (HIDARI GAMAE) – Left posture. *Leading with the left side of the body.*

HIDARI HIZA KUSSU – Left knee bent.

HIDARI JIGO TAI – Left defensive posture.

HIDARI KAGI KAMAE (HIDARI KAGI GAMAE) – Left hooking posture. *As performed in the Kata Heian Godan.*

HIDARI KOKUTSU DACHI – Left back stance.

HIDARI NANEME NI YOKERU KOTO – Left diagonal evasion.

HIDARI MAE HANGETSU DACHI – Left (leg) in front half moon stance.

HIDARI MAE HIZA KUSSU – Left front knee bent.

HIDARI MAE HIZA YAYA KUSSU – Left front knee slightly bent.

HIDARI MAE SHIZEN TAI – Left front natural position.

HIDARI MAE NEKO ASHI DACHI – Left front cat leg stance.

HIDARI RENOJI DACHI – Left L stance.

HIDARI SHIZENTAI – Left natural position, left natural stance. Feet are shoulder width apart, weight evenly distributed with the left foot moved forward. The left foot faces forward and the right foot faces 45 degrees to the right. The body also faces 45 degrees to the right.

HIDARI SOKUMEN – Left side.

HIDARI TE – Left hand.

HIDARI TEIJI DACHI – Left T stance.

HIDARI WAKI KAMAE (HIDARI WAKI GAMAE) – Left side posture.

HIDARI ZENKUTSU DACHI – Left front stance.

HIKI (HIKU) – Retract, pull back.

HIKI ASHI – Retracting leg. *Pulling the front leg back level with the other leg.*

HIKIHARAU – Clear away.

HIKI TE – The retracting hand. *Pulling the hand back after a technique to avoid being grabbed grab or in preparation for an elbow strike. Pulling and twisting the arm/hand during a technique giving balance of power to the forward moving technique. May also be used to block or pull an opponent off balance.*

HIKIYOSE – Pull near.

HIKUI – Low.

HINERI (HINERU) – Twist turn.

HINERI TENSHIN – Twist and change direction. *Executed by twisting the wrist out of the attacker's grip and simultaneously changing the direction of the body movement. As performed in the Kata Heian Sandan.*

HIZA DACHI – Kneeling stance. *As performed in the Kata Empi.*

HIZA KAMAE (HIZA GAMAE) – Knee posture. *As performed in the Kata Kanku Dai.*

HO – Step, pace.

HOKO – Direction.

HOKO TENKAN – Changing direction.

HORAN NO KAMAE (HORAN NO GAMAE) – Egg in the nest or ready posture. *Salutations where the fist in*

84

covered by the other hand and also referred to as "affection, kindness, love posture." (Jiai No Gamae) .Slight variations of this salutation is performed at the beginning and end of the Katas Bassai Dai, Jion, Jiin and Jitte. This indicates the state of mind required before beginning the Kata.

ICHI – Position, location, posture. *Also means 'one'.*

INASU – Evasion. *The is achieved by shifting the body from the line of the on coming attack.*

IPPON DACHI – One foot stance, one leg stance. *Also referred to as Ashi Dachi.*

IRIMI – To penetrate, to enter. *The action of moving closer to the opponent while defending an attack.*

JIAI NO KAMAE (JIAI NO GAMAE) – Affection, kindness and love posture. *Salutations where the fist in covered by the other hand and also referred to as "egg in the nest posture" (Horan No Gamae) .Slight variations of this salutation is performed at the beginning and end of the Katas Bassai Dai, Jion, Jiin and Jitte. This indicates the state of mind required before beginning the Kata.*

JIKU ASHI – *Pivot Leg. The supporting stationary leg when stepping from one stance into another.*

JIYU DACHI – Free stance.

JIYU KAMAE (JIYU GAMAE) – Free sparring posture.

JIYU NO KAMAE (JIYU NO GAMAE) – Freestyle on guard posture.

JODAN KAMAE (JODAN GAMAE) – Upper, high level posture.

JO SO KUTEI – Raised sole.

JUJI KAMAE (JUJI GAMAE) – Crossed arm posture.

JUN KAITEN – Regular rotation, corresponding rotation. *Where the rotation of the hips are in the same direction as the technique. e.g. Soto Uke.*

KAGI DACHI – Hook stance.

KAGI KAMAE (KAGI GAMAE) – Hooking posture. *As performed in the Kata Heian Godan (third move).*

KAHO – Downwards.

KAIKOMU – Fold, Hold under the arm.

KAISHIN – Open heart. *As performed to the Kata Kanku Dai (first move).*

KAISHU YAMA KAMAE (KAISHO YAMA GAMAE) – Open hand mountain posture, open hand wide arm posture. *As performed in the Kata Hangetsu.*

KAISHU RYOWAN KAMAE (KAISHO RYOWAN GAMAE) – Open hand wide arm (point down at 45 degrees) posture. *As performed in the Kata Hangetsu.*

KAITEN – Turn, rotate.

KAMAE (GAMAE):
(1) – Ready position of the hands. *A combative posture or stance either with or without a weapon. The stance indicate a mental attitude or frame of mind the process of "switching on".*
(2) – Kamae may also connote proper distance (Ma–ai) with respect to one's partner. *Although Kamae generally refers to a physical stance, there is an important parallel in Karate between one's physical and one's psychological bearing. Adopting a strong physical stance helps to promote the correlative adoption of a strong psychological attitude. It is*

86

important to try so far as possible to maintain a positive and strong mental bearing in Karate.

KAMAE KATA (GAMAE KATA) – Fighting stance, sparring stance (upper body).

KAMAERU – Take a posture.

KAMAE TE (GAMAE TE) – Fighting stance. *A command given by the instructor for students to get into fighting stance.*

KARIKOMI – Cutting in.

KASANERU – Pile up. *To put one on top of the other.*

KATA ASHI DACHI – Form leg stance, one leg stance. *As performed in the Kata Kanku Dai.*

KATACHI – Form.

KATA GURUMA – Shoulder wheel.

KATA HIZA DACHI – Form knee stance.

KATATE – One hand, single hand.

KAWASHI – Interaction with an opponent. *For example: the process on passing through the opponents attack, stepping in towards the attacker, while turning and evading the attack.*

KAZASU – Hold aloft.

KEAGE – Snap. *Term used to describe the 'snap' of a hand or kicking technique, when recoiled.*

KEN – Active condition, alert state. *Also means 'fist', 'closed–hand technique', 'sword' and 'tendon'.*

KIBA DACHI – Horse stance, horse riding stance, straddle–leg stance. *Legs apart with equal weight on* *both legs, feet turn in, knees turned out and hips pushed forwards. Also known as Naifanchi or Naihanchi Dachi.*

KIME (KIMI) – Decide, focus of power, finish. *The literal translation is 'decision' or 'commitment'. Concentration of spirit and mental and physical body.*

KI O TSUKE – Attention. *Musubi Dachi with open hands down both sides.*

KOHO – Rear, back direction.

KOHO KAITEN TOBI – Rear turning jump. *As performed in the Kata Empi.*

KOHO TENKAN – Reversing direction.

KOKUTSU DACHI – Back stance, Rearward lunging stance. 70% of weight on back leg with foot at 90 degrees to front leg which points forwards and with knees slightly bent. Also referred to as Gyakutsuki No Tsukomi Dachi.

KOMI – Near, against.

KOSA – Cross, crossed.

KOSA ASHI DACHI – Crossed–leg stance, crossed feet, locking stance. *Front foot is firmly on the ground with the rear foot tucked behind it with bent knees and straight back. As performed in the Kata Heian Godan (after jump). Also referred to as Kosa Dachi.*

KOSHI KAMAE (KOSHI GAMAE) – Hip posture, hip ready position. *A stance where the fists are held one above the other against one of the hips. As performed in the Kata Heian Yondan (in preparation to Yoko Geri Keage Uraken Uchi).*

KOSHIN – *Rearward.*

KOSHI NO KAITEN – Hip rotation.

KUZUSHI – Leverage.

KYODO – Movement.

MA – Distance.

MA AI – Distancing. *Distancing from one's partner and an understanding of how this may effect timing and speed of techniques for attacked and defence.*

MA AI GA TOH – Not proper distance.

MAE – Front, forward, to the front, in front of, before.

MAE ASHI – Front leg, front foot.

MAE MUKI – Facing to the front.

MAE NI ITE – Going forward.

MAE UKEMI – Forward fall, roll.

MAGERU – Bend.

MAHANMI NEKO ASHI DACHI – Half vie profile cat–leg stance.

MAKIOTOSHI – Twist–fall.

MANJI KAMAE (MANJI GAMAE) – Double block posture, swastika posture. One arm executes Gedan Barai to one side, while the other arm executes Jodan Haiwan Uke, usually carried out in Kokutsu Dachi. *As performed in the Kata Heian Godan.*

MASSUGU – Straight.

MAWARIKOMI – Circling, turning, spinning movement.

89

MAWASHI – Roundhouse.

MESUBI DACHI (MUSUBI DACHI, MOSUBI DACHI) – Informal attention stance. *Feet together with toes pointing 45° outward, arms held straight down with palms places against the thighs and fingers pointing to the ground. Toes together and heels apart.*

MIGI – Right, right–hand side. *Usually used in connection with stances.*

MIGI ASH DACHI – Right leg stance.

MIGI ASHI MAE – Right leg in front.

MIGI ASHI MAE FUSE – Right front leg take over. *Both hand and elbows are taken over the knee and the hands places on the ground turned inwards. As performed in the Kata Kanku Dai.*

MIGI ASHI MAE KOSA DACHI – Right leg in front crossed feet stance.

MIGI ASHI ORISHIKU – Right leg kneeling. *As performed in the Kata Empi.*

MIGI KAMAE (MIGI GAMAE) – Right posture. *Leading with the right side of the body.*

MIGI HIZA KUSSU – Right knee bent.

MIGI KOKUTSU DACHI – Right back stance.

MIGI MAE HANGETSU DACHI – Right (leg) in front half moon stance.

MIGI MAE HIZA KUSSU – Right front knee bent.

MIGI MAE HIZA YAYA KUSSU – Right front knee slightly bent.

MIGI MAE SHIZEN TAI – Right front natural position.

90

MIGI NANEME NI YOKERU KOTO – Right diagonal evasion.

MIGI RENOJI DACHI – Right L stance.

MIGI SHIZEN TAI – Right natural position, right natural stance. Feet are shoulder width apart, weight evenly distributed with the right foot moved forward. The right foot faces forward and the left foot faces 45 degrees to the left. The body also faces 45 degrees to the left.

MIGI SOKUMEN – Right side.

MIGI TEIJI DACHI – Right T stance.

MIGI WAKI GAMAE (MIGI WAKI KAMAE) – Right side posture.

MIGI ZENKUTSU DACHI – Right front stance.

MIZUNAGARE GAMAE (MIZO NAGARE KAMAE) – Flowing water posture.

MIZUNAGARE NO GAMAE (MIZUNAGARE NO KAMAE) – Flowing water posture. *As performed in the Kata Heian Godan.*

MODOTTE – Return to ready position.

MOROTE – Double handed, both hands, augmented.

MOROTE JO ZUKI DASHI (MOROTE JO TSUKI DASHI) – Double handed Jo staff thrusting stance.

MOROTE KOKO KAMAE (MOROTE KOKO GAMAE) – Double handed tiger mouth posture. *As performed in the Kata Empi.*

MOTO DACHI – Resulting stance, original stance. *As performed in the Kata Kanku Dai.*

MUKI – Facing.

MUSUBI DACHI (MESUBI DACHI) – **Informal attention stance.** *Feet together with toes pointing 45˚ outward, arms held straight down with palms places against the thighs and fingers pointing to the ground. Toes together and heels apart.*

NAIHANCHI DACHI (NAIFANCHI DACHI) – Horse stance, straddle leg stance with feet turned inward. *Also referred to as and Kiba Dachi.*

NANAME – Diagonally, obliquely.

NAORE – Return to Yoi.

NAO REI – Recover to attention stance. *Command given by the instructor recover to attention and prepare to bow.*

NA OTTE – Recover. *Generally the command 'Yame' is used.*

NEKO ASHI DACHI (NEKO DACHI) – Cat foot stance, Cat leg stance (cats stance). *Short stance with weight predominantly on the back leg, slightly bent and at 45 degree angle to front leg on ball of foot and with knees slightly turned in to protect groin. As performed in the Kata Hangetsu.*

NIKEITO KAMAE (NIKEITO GAMAE) – Double chicken head posture.

NOBASU (NOBASHI) – Straighten, extend.

NO KAMAE (NO GAMAE) – Guard.

NO MUKO HOFAKU – Facing opposite way.

NO TSUKOMI DACHI – Forward lunging stance.

RENOJI DACHI (REINOJI DACHI) – **L Stance.** *A stance with feet making an L shape and approximately 12* *inches (30cm) gap between heel of front foot and heel of rear foot. As performed in the Kata Heian Shodan.*

OMOTE – Front.

OROSHI – Downward.

OSAE (OSHI) – Pressing, holding.

OSHIDASU – Push out.

OSU – Push.

OTOSHI – Drop, dropping, falling.

OTOSHI HIJI ATE – Dropping elbow strike. *Elbow strike made by dropping the elbow downwards on to the target. Also referred to as Otoshi Hiji Ate.*

OTOSHI EMPI UCHI – Dropping elbow strike. *Elbow strike made by dropping the elbow downwards on to the target. Also referred to as Otoshi Empi Uchi.*

REI – Bow, respect. *The bow in Japanese culture is a mark of respect.*

RYO – Both, both sides.

RYO ASHI – Both feet, both legs.

RYOTE FUSE – Both hands facing down.

RYO KOSHI KAMAE – Both hip posture. *A stance where both clenched fists are placed on the hips (with the bottoms of the fists touching the hips).*

RYO KEN KOSHI KAMAE (RYO KEN KOSHI GAMAE) – Both fist on hips posture. *As performed in the Kata Heian Sandan.*

RYO SOKU – Both sides.

RYO SHO AWASE – Both hands together.

RYO TE – Both hands.

RYOWAN KAMAE (RYOWAN GAMAE) – Both arm posture, wide double downward block, wide arm posture. *Both arms held away from the body, point down at 45 degrees and with fists clenched to defend against a low level attack.*

RYOWAN KAMAE KAKIWAKE (RYOWAN GAMAE KAKIWAKI) – Both arm low level wedging posture, wide double downward wedging block. *Both arms held away from the body, point down at 45 degrees and with fists clenched.*

RYUSUI NO KAMAE (RYUSUI NO GAMAE) – Flowing water posture. *Similar posture to as Mizunagare No Gamae but the hand in front of the body is open with the palm facing downwards.*

RYU TE FUSE – Double hand crouch. *As performed in the Kata Kanku Dai, Kanku Sho and Unsu.*

SABAKI – Movement.

SAGI ASHI DACHI – Heron leg stance, one leg stance. *Used as preparation to Keagi Uraken in the Kata Heian Yondan. Also referred to as Gankaku Dachi or Tsuru Ashi Dachi.*

SAHO – Left direction.

SANCHIN DACHI – Hour–glass stance. *Legs are shoulder width apart with front foot turned in at 45 degree angle to back foot pointing forwards and with knees turned in to protect the groin. As performed in the Kata Nijushiho and Unsu.*

SASH ASHI – Stepping over, stepping across, extending the foot.

SASHI ASHI DACHI – Stepping across stance, extending the foot stance.

SASHITE – Raising of the hand to strike, grab, or block.

SAYU – Left and right, both sides.

SEIZA – **Formal sitting position, kneeling position.** *This requires acclimatization, but provides both a stable base and greater ease of movement than sitting cross–legged. It is used for the formal opening and closing of the class.*

SHIKO DACHI (SHEIKO DACHI) – **Square stance, split stance.** *Straddle stance with Legs apart, feet and knees turned out and hips pushed forwards. A stance often used in Goju–Ryu and Shito–Ryu.*

SHINTAI – Linear motion. *Back and forth movement, attacking and retreating.*

SHISEI – Posture, stance.

SHITA – Down. *Also means 'tongue'.*

SHITA MUKI – Facing downward.

SHITA NI – Down, under.

SHIZEN DACHI – **Natural stance.** *A term used to describe any natural stance. Also referred to as Shizentai Dachi.*

SHIZEN HONTAI – Basic natural position.

SHIZEN TAI – **Natural position.** *The body remains relaxed but alert. Feet shoulder width apart, arms by the side of the body, held approximately 4 inches away from the body and with fists clenched.*

95

SHIZENTAI DACHI – Natural stance. *Also referred to as Shizen Dachi.*

SHOMEN MUKI – Facing to the front.

SHOMEN NEKO ASHI DACHI – Front cat–leg stance, Front cat–foot stance.

SHOMEN NI MUITE – Face the front. *A command given by the instructor for students to face the official seat.*

SOCHIN DACHI – **Diagonal straddle leg stance. Rooted/immovable stance. Also referred to as Fudo Dachi. Modified front stance from the Kata Sochin.**

SOETE KOSHI KAMAE (SOETE KOSHI GAMAE) – Supporting hip posture.

SOERU – Attach.

SOKUHO – Side.

SOKUMEN – Side, flank.

SORASHI – Feint.

SORU – Sit down, kneel.

SOTO MUKI – Facing outwards.

SUBERIKOMI – Sliding in.

SUIHEI – Horizontal, level.

SUKUI – Scooping, scoop up.

SURI – Sliding.

SURI ASHI – Sliding the feet.

SUWARI – Sit. *On one's knees.*

SUWARI WAZA – Techniques from a sitting position.

TACHI:
(1) – A Japanese long sword.
(2) – Standing stance. *Also referred to as Dachi.*

TACHI HIZA – Stance knee. *As performed in the Kata Empi (first move).*

TACHIKATA – Fighting stance, sparring stance (lower body).

TACHI REI – Standing bow.

TACHI WAZA – Standing techniques.

TAIRA–NA – Level or even.

TAI – Form, body.

TAI SABAKI – Body movement, evasion, shifting direction. *One–ness of movement.*

TAOSHI – Down.

TATE – Vertical.

TATERU – Raised.

TEDORI – Hand movement.

TEIJI DACHI – T stance. *Stance with the feet in a 'T' shape' and approximately 12 inches (30cm) gap between heel of front foot and instep of rear foot. Formally called Choji Dachi.*

TENSHIN – Moving, shifting, changing course.

TOBIGOSHI – Jumping over.

TOME – Return to original position.

TOMO NI – Together.

TSUMASAKI DACHI – Crane stance, tip toe stance. *As performed in the Kata Gankaku.*

TSUGI ASHI – Following foot. *A method of moving where one foot follows the other but do not passes it.*

TSURU ASHI DACHI – **Crane leg stance. *Also referred to as Gankaku Dachi and Sagi Ashi Dachi.***

UCHI – **Inside outward. *Also means 'strike', 'strikes', 'striking', 'inside' and 'inner'.***

UCHIGAWA – Inside, inner side.

UCHI HACHIJI DACHI – **Inverted open leg stance, inverted figure eight stance.. *A natural stance, feet positioned about one shoulder width apart, with feet pointed slightly inward and arms relaxed with fists clenched.***

UE – Up on top of, above, over.

UE MUKI – Facing upwards.

UHO – Right direction.

UKE KAMAE (UKE GAMAE) – Blocking posture.

UNKOKU – Rhythm, fluidity of movement.

UNSOKU – Moving leg, leg movement.

URA – **Reverse, back, rear. *Also means 'back fist', 'upper cut'.***

URAKEN KAMAE (URAKEN GAMAE) – Back fist posture. *As performed in the Kata Hangetsu.*

URAOMOTE – Both sides, back and front.

98

URA WAZA – Reverse techniques.

USHIRO – Backward, back, rear, behind.

USHIRO MUKI – Facing to the back.

USHIRO NI ITE – Going back.

USHIRO SURI ASHI – Rear sliding leg. *The movement of the rear leg to meet the front leg.*

UYE – Up, upwards.

WAKI – Side, flank.

YAMA KAMAE (YAMA GAMAE) – Mountain Posture.

YO - Use or application of the technique. For example Bunkai, Tai-No-Sen and Go-No-Sen.

YOI DACHI – Ready stance. *This is the stance taken by karateka when the command "Yoi" is given by the instructor/sensei.*

YOKO – Side, lateral, sideward.

YOKO KAMAE (YOKO GAMAE) – Side facing posture.

YOKO KOTE GAESHI – Sideward wrist flip.

YORI ASHI – Sliding the feet, without legs crossing.

YOSE – Pulling.

ZA – Seated, kneeling.

ZA REI – The traditional Japanese bow from the kneeling position.

ZANSHIN – State of relaxed alertness, perfect posture and awareness. The state of pure and heightened mental, physical and spiritual awareness. Even after a Karate technique has been completed, one should remain in a balanced and aware state. Zanshin thus connotes "following through" in a technique, as well as preservation of one's awareness so that one is prepared to respond to additional attacks.

ZANSHIN KAMAE (ZANSHIN GAMAE) – Awareness posture.

ZA REI – Seated bow. *The traditional Japanese bow from the kneeling position.*

ZAZEN – Japanese seated meditation.

ZEMPO (ZENPO) – Front, forward.

ZENKUTSU – Forward.

ZENKUTSU DACHI – Forward stance, front stance. *Legs are shoulder width apart, the Knee of front leg over foot and rear leg locked straight. 60% of weight on front leg.*

ZENPO (ZEMPO) – Front direction.

ZENSHIN – Forward or advance

100

12

Sparring
(Kumite)

This section contains terminology relating and offensive, defensive and tactical techniques associated with sparring and combat.

組
手

AITE–NO–TSUKURI – Conditioning of the opponent. *The process of setting up ones opponent into an advantageous position where the execution of a technique would be the most effective.*

ATE – Hitting.

ATEMI JUTSU – Art of attacking vital points.

ATE WAZA – Smashing techniques, hitting techniques.

ATO UCHI – Delayed strike, feint. *Incomplete attack causing the opponent to react defensively, thus creating an alternative opening form attack.*

BO SAI KUMITE – Sparring with a staff and short weapon with two prongs.

CHOYAKU HANGEKI – Jumping counter attack.

GAESHI (KAESHI) – In wave, counter. *A counter or succession of counter attacks.*

GO NO SEN – Seizing the initiative later. *The tactic where one allows the opponent to attack first so to open up targets for counterattack.*

GOHON–KUMITE – **Five step basic sparring.** *A predetemined set of moves. The attacker steps in five consecutive times with a striking technique with each step. The defender steps back and blocks each technique. After the fifth block, the defender executes a counter–strike and Kiai.*

HYOSH – Timing.

IAI – Sparring which begins with both the attacker and the defender seated and facing each other.

IPPON KUMITE – **One step basic sparring, one step fighting.** *A formalised type of fighting where one*

102

predetermined attacks, blocks and counter strikes are executed at a time. The complexity of the attacks and counters are in accordance with the grade of student.

JISSEN – Actual Fighting.

JIYU IPPON KUMITE – **Semi freestyle sparring, free one strike sparring, free one step fighting.** *The participants can attack with any technique whenever ready.*

JIYU KUMITE (JIU KUMITE) – **Freestyle sparring, free sparring, free–form fighting.** *Controlled sparring usually in accordance with completion rules.*

KAESHI (GAESHI) – In wave, counter. *A counter or succession of counter attacks. Also referrred to as Kaesu.*

KAESHI IPPON KUMITE – Two step one attack sparring. *Reaction or returning one step sparring.*

KAESHI KUMITE – Two step sparring.

KEN NO SEN – Seizing the initiative earlier. *Attacking before the opponent attacks. Pre–emptive attack.*

KENSEI TAI (KENSEI) – Feint, The technique with silent Kiai. *Related to meditation.*

KIHON IPPON KUMITE – **Basic one step sparring.** *A predetemined set of moves. The attacker steps in with a striking technique. The defender steps back and blocks the technique and executes a counter–strike and Kiai. This is repeared for a range of Jodan and Chdan punches and Kicks.*

KIHON KUMITE – Basic sparring.

KIHON RENRAKU WAZA – Basic combination techniques.

KIRI KAESHI – Repeated counter.

103

KISHO IPPON KUMITE – Returning one step sparring.

KO BO ICHI – The concept of attack–defence connection.

KUMITACHI – Partner work.

KUZUSHI – The unbalancing of an opponent. This is either physically as in a foot sweep, mentally as in stepping on an opponent's foot before punching to distract him, or spiritually as in a fierce kiai just before an opponent attacks to "drain" his fighting spirit.

MA AI – Sparring distance. *Proper distancing or timing with respect to one's partner.*

MAAI GA TOH – Not proper distance.

ME NO TSUKEKATA – Fixing the eyes. *Looking through your opponent to aid peripheral vision.*

NI NO KOSHI NO HYOSHI – In two beats. *Attacking a second time and catching your opponent at the exact moment he relaxes after the first attack.*

NORU – To ride, to carry, to give a ride to. *The action of riding on your opponent's attacking arm or leg etc.*

OKURI JIYU IPPON KUMITE – Two Step free sparing. *Two step one attack sparring, second step free.*

OYO WAZA – Applications interpreted from techniques in Kata.

RANDORI – Free for all fighting. *Free–form fighting without rules or fighting in Judo.*

REN – Consecutive punches, consecutive kicks. *See Ren Zuki and Ren Geri.*

RENRAKU – Combinations. *In relation to fighting combinations.*

104

RENRAKU WAZA – Combination techniques. *Multiple attacks and defences performed in succession.*

SANBON KUMITE – **Three step sparring.** *Usually a series of three preditermined different attacks. The attacker steps in three consecutive times with a striking technique with each step. The defender steps back and blocks each technique. After the third block, the defender executes a counter–strike and Kiai.*

SEN – Initiative. *Positive action taken when in a comcative situation.*

SEN NO SEN – Seizing the initiative first. *Attacking at the exact moment when the opponent attacks.*

SEN SEN NO SEN – Pre–emptive attack. *Attacking before the opponent attacks.*

SHIZEN KUMITE – Natural sparring.

SUTEMI WAZA – Last chance technique.

TAIMING GA OSOI – Not correct timing.

TAI NO SEN – Seizing the initiative earlier. *To charge into the attack and to penetrate the enemy by force.*

TAI–TAI NO SEN – Seizing the initiative earlier and later.

TAMERAU - Hesitate.

TEN NO KATA – Kata of the universe/heaven. *Formal exercise created by Gichin Funakoshi and designed to facilitate the understanding of kumite.*

TORRE – Attacker.

TSUKURI – Creating an opening in your defence to draw the opponent into a specific attack and this allowing you to respond with a specific counterattack.

YAKUSOKU KUMITE – Predetermined sparring. *The opposite of Jiyu kumite.*

YU NO SEN – Seizing the initiative later. *To test the opponents defences by shifting and changing posture in order to create an opening and then to take initiative to and attack.*

13

Vital Points & The Body
(Jintai Kyusho To Karada)

This section contains anatomical terminology relating parts of the body, parts of the body used as weapons, target areas and vital points.

人体急所と体

107

AGO – Chin, jawbone.

AKIRESU KEN – Achilles tendon.

ASHI – Foot, leg.

ASHIBO – Shin

ASHI GATANA – Foot sword. *A reaping technique like a sword stroke. The foot to the outside or inside.*

ASHI JOSOKUTEI – Ball of the foot.

ASHIKO – Instep.

ASHIKUBI – Ankle, foot joint.

ASHI NO URA (**ASHI URA**) – Sole of the foot.

ASHI SOKUTO – Outer edge 'knife edge' of the foot.

ASHIYUBI – Toes, foot digit.

ASHI ZOKO – Bottom/underside of foot.

ATAMA – Head, top of the head.

AWASE HIKI TSUKAMI – Combined pulling grasp. *As performed in the Kata Heian Godan.*

AWASE KOKO UKE – Combined tiger mouth block. *As performed in the Kata Empi.*

AWASE (MAWASHI) KAKE–UKE – Combined roundhouse hooking block. *As performed in the Kata Nijushiho.*

AWASE MAWASHI UKE – Combined roundhouse block. *As performed in the Kata Kanku Dai.*

AWASE SHUTO AGE UKE – Combined knife hand rising block. *As performed in the Kata Chinte.*

108

AWASE UKE – **Combined/combination block, joined hand block.**

BISEN – Bridge of nose.

BITE – Head of nose.

BITEI – Base of the spine. *Vital point.*

BITO – Head of nose.

CHI – Blood.

CHICHI – Nipple.

CHIBUSA – Breast.

CHUDAN – Middle area of body e.g. chest and stomach.

CHUKITSU – Side of elbow joint. *Vital point. Also referred to as Hijizume.*

CHUSOKU – Ball of the foot.

DANCHU – Top of sternum, pit of neck. *Vulnerable point for attack.*

DENKO – Upper side abdominal region. *Vital point between the seventh and eighth ribs.*

DO – Torso, truck of the body. *Also means 'way', 'path of life', 'movement' and 'activity'.*
DOKKO – Behind the ear. *Vital point.*

EMPI – Elbow. *Also referred to as Hiji.*

EN SHO – Round heel, heel of foot. *Also referred to as Kakato.*

ERIKUBI – Collar beck, side of neck.

FUKURAHAGI – Calf of the leg.

109

FUKUTO – Outside of the lower thigh. *Vital point.*

FUSHI – Joint, knuckle.

FUSHITO – Outside of thigh.

GAIWAN – Outer arm, outside of the forearm. *Part of the forearm located on the side opposite the thumb. Used for blocking as in Soto Uke.*

GAN – Eye. *Also referrred to as Gansei.*

GANCHU – Area below the nipples.

GANKA – Area of chest below the nipples. *Vital point.*

GANKYU/GANSEI – Eyeballs/eyeball.

GANMEN KOGEGI – Attack to the face with a hand or elbow. *This is not permitted in completion and is considered a foul (Hansoku).*

GANSEI – Eyeball. *Vital point.*

GANSHU – Under nipples.

GEDAN – Lower area of body. Groin or generally below the waste.

GEKON – Lower jaw, beneath lower lip. *Vital point.*

GENKOTSU – Attacking vital points.

GOSHI (KOSHI) – Hip.

HA – Tooth.

HADASHI – Bare feet.

HADA – Skin. *Also referred to as Hifu.*

110

HAGUKI – Gums.

HAI – Lung.

HAISHU (HAISHO, HAESHU) – **Back of flat hand, back–hand.**

HAIWAN – **Back arm.** *Upper side of the forearm.*

HAIBU – Back area.

HANA – Nose.

HARA – Stomach, Abdomen, Centre. *Abdominal life/death energy centre located in the stomach. The position around the stomach which is believed to be the seat of the soul in the eastern martial arts and the source of Ki (Chi).*

HATO MUNE – Sternum.

HAYAUCHI – Edge of shoulder blades. *Vital point.*

HEISOKU (HAISOKU) – Instep of the foot. *Top of the foot beteen shin anfd toes.*

HICHU – Windpipe. *Base of neck central between the collar bones. Vital point.*

HIDARITE – Left hand.

HIFU – Skin. *Also referred to as Hada.*

HIIRU – Heel.

HIJI – Elbow. *Also referred to as Empi.*

HIJIZUME – Side of elbow joint. *Vital point. Also referred to as Chukitsu.*

HIRA KOTE – Level forearm.

111

HIRATE – Inside of the hand.

HITAI – Forehead, brow.

HITOSASHIYUBI – Index finger.

HITTSUI (HITSUI) – Knee. *Also refurred to as Hiza.*

HIZA – Knee or lap. *Also refurred to as Hittsui.*

HIZAGASHIIRA – Knee

HIZAKANSETSU – Knee joint.

HIZA TSUBOMI – Back of knee.

HONE – Bone. *Also refers to ribs and skeletal frame.*

HOO – Cheek.

I – Stomach.

ICHI BYOSHI – In one breath

INAZUMA – Side of stomach.

ISSHI KEN – Extended index finger.

JINCHU – Philtrum. *Vital point at the base of the nose under and between the nostrils.*

JINTAI KYUSHO – Vital Points. *Particularly sensitive parts of the body where a blow or applied pressure would incapacitate the opponent.*

JINZO – Kidney.

JODAN – Upper Area of body e.g. face and head.

JOGAKU – Upper part of jaw.

JOMYAKU – Vein.

JOTAI – Upper body.

JUNZO – Kidneys.

KACHIKAKE – Point of the jaw. *Also referred to as Ago.*

KA FUKU BU – Lower abdomen.

KAGAKU – Lower part of jaw.

KAHANSHIN – Lower half of the body.

KAKATO – Heel of foot, round heel. *Also referred to as En Sho.*

KAKUTO – Heel of hand, bent wrist.

KAMINOKE (KAMI) – Hair. *Also referred to as Ke.*

KANSETSU – Joint, knuckles. *Also means 'joint lock'.*

KANZO – Liver. *Also referred to as Kimo.*

KAO – Face.

KARADA – Body, physique.

KASSATSU – The spine between the shoulder blades. *Vital point.*

KASUMI – Temple, side of the head. *Vital point. Also referred to as Komekami).*

KATA – Shoulder. *Also means 'form'.*

KATAGUCHI – Shoulder.

KATSUSATSU (KASUSATSU) – Spot between 5th – 6th vertebrae.

KAU – Face.

KE– Hair. Also referred to as Kami and Kaminoke.

KEICHU – Back of neck, nape of neck at base of skull. *Vital point.*

KEIDO MYAKU – Jugular vein.

KEIKO – Joined Fingertips, chicken beak hand. *Also means 'training', 'practice' and 'drill'.*

KEKKAN – Blood vessel.

KEN – Tendon, fist. *Also means 'closed–hand technique', 'sword', 'active condition', 'alert state'.*

KENTEKI – Testicles, groin.

KETTO – Blood.

KIBI – Tip of spine.

KINNIKU – Muscle.

KINTEKI – Testicles. *Vital point.*

KO – Back of fist, back of hand.

KOBORE – Tibia.

KODENKO – Base of spine.

KOHO – Back, behind, rear.

KOKEI – Tibia bone.

KOKEN – Wrist joint, bent wrist.

KOKOTSU – Shin bone. *Vital point. Also referred to as Mukozune.*

114

KOMEKAMI (KOMIKAMI) – Temple Area, side of the head. *Vital point. Also referred to as Kasumi.*

KORI – Instep. *Vital point. Upper surface of the instep.*

KOSHI:
(1) – Ball of the foot.
(2) – Hip, waist, side. Pelvic carriage. The pelvis and surrounding structures. Indicates the hip area.

KOTE – Forearm, wrist, back–hand.

KOTOBU – Rear of head.

KUBI – Neck.

KUCHI – Mouth.

KUCHIBIRU – Lip.

KURUBUSHI – Ankle.

KUSANAGI – Lower part of calf muscle. *Vital point.*

KUSAGAKURE – Outter edge of the top of the foot. *Vital point. Also referred to as Soin.*

KYOBU – Chest.

KYOEI – Under the arms in line with then nipples between the 5th and 6th ribs. *Vital points.*

KYOSEN – Lower part of the sternum, upper solar plexus. *Vital point.*

KYOTOTSU – Base of sternum.

KYUSHO – Vital points, pressure points.

KYUSHO WAZA – Vital point techniques.

115

MATA – Top of the thigh.

MAEUDE – Forearm, wrist.

MATSUKAZE – The side of the neck. *Vital point.*

MAYU – Eyebrow.

ME – Eye, eyes.

MEN – Face, side, surface.

MENSUKI – Head.

MIGITE – Right hand.

MIKAZUKI – Lower jaw bone. Ridge of the lower jaw. *Vital point. Also means 'crescent moon', 'new moon'.*

MIKEN – Summit of the nose in the centre of the forehead.

MIMI – Ear, ears.

MITEN – Bridge of nose.

MIYAKUDOKORO – Inner parts of the forearm. *Where the pulse can be felt. Also referred to as Uchijakuzawa.*

MIZO OCHI – Solar plexus.

MOMO – Thigh.

MUKOZUNE – Shin bone. *Vital point. Also referred to as Kokotsu.*

MUNE – Chest, abdomen.

MURASAME – Clavicle. *Base of throat above the collar bones. Vital points.*

MYOJO – Lower abdomen, 2.5cm below navel. *Vital point.*

116

NAIKE – Inside surface of the ankle. *Vital point. Also referred to as Uchikurubushi.*

NAIWAN – Inner arm. *Inner side of the forearm. Used for blocking as in Uchiuke.*

NIKU – Flesh.

NODO – Throat.

NODO BOTOKE – Adam's Apple.

NOGO – Throat.

OMOTE KOTE – Front forearm, inner forearm.

ONAKA – Stomach.

OYAYUBI – Thumb.

OYAYUBI IPPON KEN – Thumb knuckle.

ROKKOTSU – Rib, ribs.

RYOJIKOU KABOTOKE – Mastoid.

SAKOTSU – Collar bone.

SEBONE – Spine, backbone.

SEIDON – Areas below and above eyes. *Vital point*.

SEIKA TANDEN – Lower abdomen.

SEISHOKUKI – Genitals.

SENAKA – Back of body.

SEOI – Shoulder.

SHIGETSU – Solar plexus.

SHINE KEITO – Nervous system.

SHINKEI – Nerves.

SHINTAI – Body.

SHINZO – Heart.

SHIRI – Hip.

SHITA – Tongue. *Also means 'down'.*

SHITAHARA – Lower abdomen.

SHITSUTO – Knee cap.

SHO – **Palm of the hand,** *open hand. Also means 'small',* *'minor'.*

SHOFU – Side of neck.

SHOMEN (SHOMON) – **Front or top of head.** *Also means 'place of honour', 'founder', 'front', 'forward'.*

SHO TEKUBBI – Hand and wrist.

SHOTAI (SHOTEI, SHOTE) – **Palm of Hand, palm heel.** *The palm of the hand when the fingers are drawn back.* *Also refured to as Taisho.*

SHUKO – Back of the hand. *Vital points.*

SHU WAN – **Lower arm, palm arm.**

SOBI – Lower part of calf muscle.*The area on the inside of the lower part of the leg, near the base of the calf.*

SODA – Spot between shoulder blades.

SOIN – Top of the foot. *Vital point. Also referred to as Kusagakure.*

SOKKO – Top of the foot.

SOKUMEN – Side, side of the face.

SOKUTEI – Sole of foot.

SOKUTO – Edge of foot, knife–edge of the foot. The striking area in a side thrust or snap kick.

SONU – Top of sternum. *Area between the throat and top of the breastbone or sternum.*

SOTOJAKUZAWA – Outer part of the forearm. *Where the pulse can be felt.*

SOTOSHAKUTAKU – Back of upper wrist. *Vital point.*

SOWAN – Both arms.

SUASHI – Bare foot.

SUHADA – Bare skin.

SUIGETSU – Solar Plexus. *Vital point.*

SUJI – Muscle fibre.

SUNE – Shin.

TAI – Body.

TAIKAKU – Build, physique, body shape.

TAI SOKU NI – To the side of the body.

TANCHU – Upper part of the sternum. *Vital point.*

TANDEN – Lower Abdomen, Stomach. *Location of the body's centre of gravity.*

TATEKEN – Vertical fist.

TE – Hand. This is the Te in Karate, Shuri-Te To-Te referring to the hand technieqes use in Japanese and Okinawan syles of martial arts.

TEKUBI – Wrist, forearm.

TENDO – Top of head, crown of head. *Vital point.*

TENTO – Frontal area of the head. *Vital point. The space between the crown of the head and the forehead.*

TOBU – Head area, excluding the face.

TOMOE – Stomach. *Also means 'circular'.*

TSUMASAKI – Tips of fingers and toes.

TSUME – Nail of the fingers or toes. *Used to cut across the opponents eyes.*

UBI – Fingers.

UCHIJAKUZAWA – Inner parts of the forearm. *Where the pulse can be felt. Also referred to as Miyakudokoro.*

UCHIKURUBUSHI (UCHIKUROBUSHI) – Inside surface of the ankle, inside of the ankle joint. *Vital point. Also referred to as Naike.*

UCHI SHAKUTAKU – Inside wrist. *Vital point.*

UCHITE – Striking hand.

UDE KANSETSU – Forearm joint, arm joint.

UDE – Arm.

UHAI TEKUBI – Back of right wrist.

USHIRO DENKO – Lower back either side of the spine. *Vital points.*

120

USHIRO INAZUMA – Spot below buttocks. *Vital point.*

UTO – Bridge of the nose between the eyes. *Vital point.*

WAKI – Side of chest, flank.

WAKIBARA – Side of the chest.

WAKI NO SHITA – Armpit.

WAN – Arm.

WANJUN – Upper arm between biceps and triceps. *Vital point.*

WANSHUN – Back of upper arm. Top of outside edge of upper arm.

YOBO – Face.

YAKO – The inside of the upper thigh. *Vital point.*

YUBI – Finger, toe.

YUBI NO KANSETSU – Knuckle.

YUBISAKI – Fingertip.

ZENSHIN – Whole body, entire body.

ZENWAN – Forearm.

ZUNO – Head. Also Brains.

14

Form
(Kata)

This section contains the names and translated meanings of the 26 Shotokan Kata, terminology used in connection with Kata and influential Kata performed by other styles.

型

BASSAI – To storm a fortress, to storm a castle, to penetrate a fortress. *The kata now comes in two forms, Bassai Dai and Bassai Sho. Dai being the major version and Sho the lesser or minor version. There are however many variations. The Kata are currently practised by Shotokan and Wado Ryu.*

BASSAI DAI – **Brown belt level Kata, translated as "To Penetrate a Fortress Major" or "To Storm the Castle".** *The exact origins of Bassai Dai are unknown. The kata was practised by Shuri Te and there is some evidence to suggest it was practised by Tomari Te.*

BASSAI SHO – **Shodan level Kata, translated as "To Penetrate a Fortress Minor" or "To Storm the Castle and Capture the Enemy".** *Bassai Sho was created in more recent times by Master Itotsu.*

BUNKAI – **Practical Application, Application of Kata.** *A study of and application of Kata movements. The practice of applying specific techniques to real situations.*

CHINTE – **Nidan level Kata meaning "Extra–ordinary (strange/unusual) hands", "chinese hands".** *The Kata was originally know as Shoin and is of Chinese origin. Apparently Master Funakoshi refered to this Kata as Shoin but it is thought that the name is a refelection of the Chinese influence. Currently practised by Shotokan.*

CHINTO – An Okinawan Shorin Ryu Kata, meaning fighting to the east. *Later changed to Gankaku by Master Funakoshi. The Kata was originally named after famous Chinese sailor who was shipwrecked on the shores of Okinawa and who influenced the early development of Te.*

EMBUSEN – Floor pattern of a given Kata, performance line.

EMPI (ENPI) – **Brown Belt level Kata, translated as "The Flight of a Swallow" or "Flying Swallow".** *Originally called Wanshu but the name was changed by Gichin*

Funakoshi. The Kata was practised by Master Itosu and is believed to originate from Shuri Te. The Kata is currently practised by Shotokan.

GANKAKU – Nidan level Kata translated as "Crane standing on a rock". *The Kata was formally known as Chinto after the originator who is believed to be the Chinese military attache. The kata contains techniques for attacking the vital points. The Kata was practised by*

both Tomari Te and Shuri Te and is currenly practised by Shotokan, Shito Ryu and Wado Ryu.

GOJUSHIHO – Sandan level Kata translated as 54 steps. Originally an Okinawain Kata named Hotaku with 54 moves. *Previous names were Ouseishi, Useshi, Hotaku. The Kata come in two forms, Gojushiho–Dai and Gojushiho–Sho, Dai being the major version and Sho the lesser or minor version. The kata is believed to have developed through Shuri Te and taught to Sensei Funakoshi by Master Itosu. Sensei Kenwa Mabuni the creator of Shito Ryu, perfected the kata and called it Useshi. The kata is currently practised by Shotokan and Shito Ryu.*

GOJUSHIHO DAI – Sandan level Kata translated as 54 steps minor. Originally an Okinawain Kata named Hotaku with 54 moves.

GOJUSHIHO SHO – Sandan level Kata translated as 54 steps major. Originally an Okinawain Kata named Hotaku with 54 moves.

HAKKO – The original name for the Kata Sochin.

HANGETSU (HUNGETSU) – Brown belt level Kata translated as "Half Moon" or "Crescent Moon". *Previous names were Seishan, Seisan. The Kata requires a tense body from the inside out allowing the energy to flow through the body to the arm or fist. The Kata originates from NahaTe and is currently* *practised by Shotokan, Goju Ryu, Uechi Ryu and Wado Ryu.*

HEIAN – Series of 5 Kata. Heian meaning peaceful mind, taken from the city of Heian. *Originally known by the Okinawan name Pinan and still referred as this name by many styles of Karate. Currently practised by Shotokan, Wado Ryu and Shito Ryu.*

HEIAN GODAN – **Kata, translated as "peaceful mind fifth level".**

HEIAN NIDAN – **Kata, translated as "peaceful mind second level".**

HEIAN SANDAN – **Kata, translated as "peaceful mind third level".**

HEIAN SHODAN – **Kata, translated as "peaceful mind first level".**

HEIAN YONDAN – **Kata, translated as "peaceful mind fourth level"**

HEISHUGATA (HEISHUKATA, HEISOGUTA) – Kata performed while under constant tension. *As performed in the Kata Sanchin.*

HOTAKU – The original name for the Kata Gojushiho Dai & Sho.

IBUKI – Controlled breathing.

JIIN – **Nidan level Kata, translated as "Temple Grounds".** *Previous known as Shokyo. Another Kata believed to have come from Chinese temple of Join Ji and this is re–inforced by the Chinese salutation Jiai no kamae at the start and finish of the kata. The Kata is thought to have had Tomari Te origins although the kata is also known to have been practised by Shuri Te. The kata is The Kata is currently practised by Shotokan.*

JION – Brown belt level Kata, name is believed to be taken from the Buddhist temple of "Jion" in China. *This is theory strengthened by the salutation at the start and finish. Originally a Shorei Ryu Kata that came from China. The kata is known to have been practised by Shuri Te and Tomari Te and is curently practised by Shotokan, Shito Ryu and Wado Ryu.*

JITTE – Shodan level Kata, translated as "Ten hands". *The title emplies when you have mastered the Kata and you will attain the skils to defeat ten men. This falls into the Shorei–Ryu category of Kata and was previously known as Jutte. As a Shotokan Kata it is uneque as it contains no punches. The kata is thought to be from Tomari Te and also known to have been practised by Shuri Te. The salutation at the start and finish of the kata suggests Chinese origins and like Jion may have been practised at the Jion Je temple. The Kata is curently practised by Shotokan, Wado Ryu and Shito Ryu.*

KAISHU KATA (KAISHUGATA, KAISUGATA) – Kata performed in a semi–relaxed state. *Speed and focus as techniques are executed.*

KANKU – "To view the sky", "watching the sky", "look at the sky". *Other earlier name for the Kata were Koshokun, Kushanku, Kwanku and Shankyu. The kata now comes in two forms, Kanku Dai and Kanku Sho. Dai being the major version and Sho the lesser or minor version. The kata are practised by Shotokan, Shorin Ryu, Shito Ryu and Wado Ryu.*

KANKU DAI – Brown belt level Kata, translated as "Viewing the Sky Major" or "To Look at the Sky Major". *The kata originates from Shuri–te and it is believed that the Chinese Military Attache to Okinawa (highly skilled exponent of Kempo), Kume Mura Kong–Shang (Kushanku to the Okinawans) taught the kata under the name Kwanku to his students Tode Sakagawa and Yari.*

KANKU SHO – **Shodan level Kata, translated as "Viewing the Sky Minor" or "To Look at the Sky Minor".** *Kanku Sho was created in more recently by Master Itosu.*

KATA – Form, shape, style, model. *Formal prescribed pattern of movement. A series of predetermined blocks, punches, strikes, kicks and breaks etc. Also means 'shoulder'.*

KUSANKU – An Okinawan Shorin Ryu Kata. *Named after a Chinese Master and government official.*

MEIKYO – **Sandan level Kata translated as "Bright polished mirror" or "Vision of a white heron".** *Previous names were Rohai, Lorei. The Kata is known to have been practised by both Tomari Te and Shuri Te and is currently practised by Shotokan and Wado Ryu.*

NAGORE – Deep breathing.

NAIHANCHI (NAIFANCHI) – The original Okinawan name for the Kata Tekki, translated as "fighting on the dikes between rice paddies" or "inside fighting."

NIJUSHIHO – **Shodan level Kata. The name is derived from the 24 foot movements performed in the Kata.** *Originally named Niseshi, Neseishi. The Kata is known to have been practised by Tomari–te and is currently practised by Shotokan, Shito Ryu and Wado Ryu.*

OYO WAZA – Applications interpreted from Kata techniques.

PASSAI – An Okinawan Shorin Ryu Kata. *Meaning is unknown.*

PINAN – **A series of five Kata formulated by Okinawan Master Yatsutsune Itosu (better known as Anko Itosu).**

ROHAI – Older version of the Kata Meikyo.

SANCHIN – Goju Ryu Kata. *Created by Chojun Miyagi and emphasises strong form and breath control.*

128

SEIPAI – An Okinawan Shorei Ryu Kata.

SEISAN – An Okinawan Shorin Ryu Kata. Translated as "Thirteen."

SOCHIN – **Nidan level Kata meaning "strength and calmness".** *Also mean immovable in the face of danger, to root, to suppress, to preserve the peace, old man fighting and the grand prize. Mainly performed in Sochin Dachi and once known as Hakko. It is believed to have been passed down through Ankichi Aragaki from Tomari–te.*

TAIKYOKU – First cause. *Series of three Kata developed by Gichin and Yoshitaka Funakoshi for beginners. Also referred as Kihon, these are the first Kata taught in main Shotokan schools of Karate. Funakoshi said that if a student understood the concepts of the Taikyoku Kata, then he should understand the idea that you begin with basics and return to basics.*

TAIMING GA OSOI – Not proper timing.

TEKKI:
(1) – Series of 3 Kata of Chinese origins. *Translated as "Iron Horse" or "Horse riding". Originally a single Kata named Naihanchi. Naihanchi is known to have been practised since ancient times by Naha Te and Shuri Te, being influenced by Master Itosu. The Kata belonging to the Shuri Te style and is currently practised by Shotokan, Wado Ryu and Shito Ryu.*
(2) – Spiked metal knuckledusters.

TEKKI SHODAN – **Kata, translated as "Iron Horse first level" or "Horse riding first level".**

TEKKI NIDAN – **Kata, translated as "Iron Horse first level" or "Horse riding second level".**

TEKKI SANDAN – **Kata, translated as "Iron Horse first level" or "Horse riding third level".**

TEN NO KATA – Shotokai Kata created. Designed under the leadership and guidance of Funakoshi.

UNSU – Sandan level Kata meaning "cloud–hands" or "hands in the clouds". *Believed to be the kata's original name. The Kata is known to have been practised by Tomari Te and is currently practised by Shotokan, Wado Ryu and Shito Ryu.*

WANKAN – Sandan level Kata translated as "Kings Crown", "Crown of Kings", "Pine tree wind". *This Kata only has one Kiai. Previous names were Shiofu, Hito, Okan and Matsukase. The katas origin is through Matsumora to Tomari–te. It cutrently practiced by Shotokan, Wado Ryu and Shito Ryu although there are great differences between the versions.*

WANSHU – An Okinawan Shorin Ryu Kata named after a Chinese Master. *The original name for the Kata Empi. The name of this traditional Okinawan Kata was changed by Gichin Funakoshi.*

15

Competition Terminology
(Shobu Yogo)

This section contains phases and terminology use in competition and associated with competitive events.

勝
負
用
語

AITE – Opponent in contest.

AI UCHI – Simultaneous strike/scoring technique. *This may be stated by the referee in Kumite competition. He brings his fists together in front of his chest. No point is awarded to either contestant.*

AKA – Red (competitor on right).

AKA [SHIRO] NO KACHI – Red [white] wins. *The referee obliquely raises his arm on the side of the winner.*

AKA [SHIRO] IPPON – Red [white] scores Ippon. *The referee obliquely raises his arm on the side of the winner.*

ANA TA NO KACHI – You are the winner.

ATENAI YONI – **Warning without penalty.** *This phrase may be used by the referee in Kumite competition. He raises one hand in a fist with the other hand covering it at chest level and shows it to the offender. A warning may be imposed for attended minor infractions or for the first instance of a minor infraction.*

ATOSHI BARAKU – A little more time left. *This is a phrase used in Kumite competition. An audible signal will be given by the time keeper 30 seconds before the actual end of the bout.*

ATTATE IRU – Contact.

AWAZA TE IPPON – Makes a full point.

CHUI – Warning.

CHUI ICHI – First warning.

CHUI NI – Second warning. *In completion this will result in the fist penalty.*

132

ENCHO SEN – Extra time. *Extension of a competition match after a draw. The match goes into overtime and the referee re-opens the bout with command "Shobu Hajime."*

FUKUSHIN (FUKASHIN) – Judge, judges.

FUKUSHIN SHUGO (FUKASHIN SHUGO) – Judge come here! *Call to judges for a conference.*

GENTEN – Penalty.

GENTEN ICHI – First penalty.

GENTEN NI – Second penalty. *In completion this will result in disqualification.*

HANSOKU – Foul, violations of rules. *This may be imposed by the referee in Kumite competition as he points with his index finger to the face of the offender at a 45 degree angle and announces a victory for the opponent. This is imposed following a very serious infraction. It results in the opponent's score being raised to Sanbon. Hansoku is also invoked when the number of Hansoku–Chui and Keikoku imposed raise the opponent's score to Sanbon.*

HANSOKU CHUI – Warning with a point penalty (awarded to opponent. *This is a phrase used by the referee in Kumite competition as he points with his index finger to the abdomen of the offender parallel to the floor. This is a penalty in which Ippon is added to the opponent's score. Hansoku–Chui is usually imposed for infractions for which a Keikoku has previously been given in that bout.*

HANTEI – Judgment, decision, referee and judges' verdict. *In competition where no full point has been scored or disqualification the referee calls for judgment by blowing his whistle and the judge's render their decision by flag signal.*

HANTEI KACHI – Winner by decision.

133

HIKIWAKE – Draw. *This may be announced by the referee in Kumite competition. He crosses his arms over his chest and then uncrosses them and holds them out from the body with palms facing down.*

IPPON – One full point. *This may be announced by the referee in Kumite competition as he raises his arm upwards at 45 degrees on the side of the scorer. One point may be awarded for a single technique or as the result of two half points (two Waza Ari) techniques.*

IPPON SHOBU – One point match, used in tournaments. *One full point (one Ippon) or two half points (two Waza Ari) to win the contest.*

JIKAN – Time. *As in tournament.*

JOGAI – Out of bounds, exit from the fighting area. *This may be stated by the referee in Kumite competition. He points with his index finger to the match boundary on the side of the offender. It is not permitted to exit from fighting area in competition and is considered a foul (Hansoku).*

JOGAI CHUI – Out of bounds warning for an exit from the fighting area. *This may be stated by the referee in Kumite competition. He points with his index finger to the match boundary on the side on the side of the offender and then points with his index finger to the abdomen of the offender. It is not permitted to exit from fighting area in completion.*

JOGAI KEIKOKU – Out of bounds warning with Waza Ari penalty for second exit from the fighting area. *This may be imposed by the referee in Kumite competition. He points with his index finger to the match boundary on the side on the side of the offender and then points with his index finger to the abdomen of the offender. Second exit from fighting area and a Waza Ari penalty is given to the opponent. It is not permitted to exit from fighting area in competition.*

134

JOGAI HANSOKU – Out of bounds foul with a Sanbon penalty for forth exit from the fighting area. *This may be imposed by the referee in Kumite competition. He points with his index finger to the match boundary on the side on the side of the offender and then points with his index finger to the abdomen of the offender and announces victory to his opponent "Aka (Shiro) Nokachi". This is a penalty in which Sanbon is added to the opponent's score. It is not permitted to exit from fighting area in completion.*

JOGAI HANSOKU CHUI – Out of bounds foul warning with Ippon penalty for third exit from the fighting area. *This may be stated by the referee in Kumite competition. He points with his index finger to the match boundary on the side on the side of the offender and then points with his index finger to the abdomen of the offender and announces "Aka (Shiro) Jogai Hansoku Chui". This is a penalty in which Ippon is added to the opponent's score. It is not permitted to exit from fighting area in completion.*

KAKAEKOMI – Hugging. *This is not permitted in completion and is considered a foul (Hansoku).*

KAKENIGE – Retreating, back off, failing to attack. *This is not permitted in competition and is considered a foul (Hansoku).*

KAKOKU – Personal warning.

KEIKOKU – Warning with Waza Ari penalty. *This is announced by the referee in Kumite competition as he points with his index finger to the feet of the offender at an angle of 45 degrees. This is a penalty in which a half point (Waza Ari) is added to the opponent's score. Keikoku is imposed for minor infractions for which a warning has previously been given in that bout, or for infractions not sufficiently serious enough to merit Hansoku–Chui.*

KIKEN – Retirement through injury, withdrawal, renunciation. *This may be announced by the referee in Kumite competition. He points with his index finger*

towards the renouncing contestant giving victory to the opponent.

MIENAI – I could not see, not seen by referee or judge. *A call by a judge to indicate that a given technique was not visible from his/her angle.*

MOTO NO ICHI – Original position. *This is a phrase used in Kumite competition. The competitors, referee and judge return to their respective standing lines.*

MUBOBI (MUMOBI) – **Warning for lack of regard for ones own safety.** *This may be imposed by the referee in Kumite competition as he points one finger in the air at a 60 degree angle on the side of the offender.*

MUBOBI KEIKOKU (MUMOBI KEIKOKU) – Warning for lack of regard for ones own safety with Waza Ari penalty. *This may be imposed by the referee in Kumite competition. Referee uses two hand signals with announcement "Aka (Shiro) Mubobi Keikoku". He first points with his index finger at a 60 ° angle on the side of the offender, then to the offender's feet.*

MUMOBI KEIKOKU – Warning with Waza Ari penalty. *Referee uses two hand signals with announcement Aka (Shiro) Mubobi Keikoku. He first points with his index finger at a 60 ° angle on the side of the offender, then to the offender's feet.*

NIHON SHOBU – Two point match, used in tournaments. *Two full point (two Ippon) or four half points (four Waza Ari) to win the contest.*

NO KACHI – Victorious, winner. *This is a phrase used by the referee in Kumite completion as the referee raises his arm at 45 degrees on the side of the winner thus announcing the winner to be red or white (e.g. "Aka No Kachi").*

SANBON SHOBU – Three point match, used in tournaments. *Three full points (three Ippon) or six half points (six Waza Ari) to win the contest.*

SHIAI – Match, contest, tournament.

SHIAIJO – Contest area.

SHIKKAKU (SHIKAKU) – **Disqualification, expulsion from even.** *This may be imposed by the referee in Kumite competition. The referee uses two hand signals with the announcement "Aka (Shiro) Shikkaku" and first points with his index to the offender's face then obliquely above and behind him. The Referee will announce with the appropriate gesture as previously given "Aka (Shiro) No Kachi". This is a disqualification from the tournament, competition or match. The opponent's score is raised to Sanbon. In order to define the limit of Shikkaku the referee council must be consulted. Shikkaku may be invoked when a contestant commits an act which harms the prestige and honour of Karate–Do and when other actions are considered to violate the rules of the tournament.*

SHIRO – **White (competitor on left).**

SHIRO [AKA] NO KACHI – White [red] wins. *The referee obliquely raises his arm on the side of the winner.*

SHIRO [AKA] IPPON – White [red] scores Ippon. *The referee obliquely raises his arm on the side of the winner.*

SHITEI – Compulsory Kata.

SHOBU – **Contest, match, competition.**

SHOBU HO – **Contest rules.**

SHOBU HAJIME – **Start the extended match.** *This is a command used by the referee in Kumite competition as he stands on his line.*

SHOBU SANBON HAJIME – **Two point completions begin, start the match, begin the bout.** *This is a* *command used by the referee in Kumite competition as he stands on his line.*

SHOTEI OSHI – Pushing the opponent with open hands. *This is not permitted in completion and is considered a foul (Hansoku).*

SHUGO – Judges Called. *The referee beckons with his arms to the judges in case of Shikkaku decision.*

SHUSHIN:
(1) – Decision of the judges.
(2) – Referee

SHUSHIN NI REI – Bow to judges. *A command given by the instructor for students to face the judges and bow.*

SOREMADE – End of bout.

TOKUI – Favourite, free choice. As in optional Kata in competition.

TONO NO ICHI – Return to your positions.

TORANAI – No Point.

TORIMASEN – Unacceptable as scoring techniques, no score. *This may be stated by the referee in Kumite competition. He crosses his arms over his chest and then uncrosses them and holds them out from the body with palms facing down.*

TSUKAMI – Grabbing. *Grabbing the opponent's Gi is not permitted in completion and is considered a foul (Hansoku).*

TSUZUKETE – Fight on! *Resumption of fighting ordered when unauthorized interruption occurs.*

TSUZUKETE HAJIME – Resume fighting – Begin. *This phrase may be used by the referee in Kumite competition. He stands on his line, steps back into Zenkutsu Dachi and brings the* *palms on his hands towards each other with elbows remaining straight.*

WAZA ARI – Half point. *This may be announced by the referee in Kumite competition as he extends his arm downwards at 45 degrees on the side of the scorer. Half a point is awarded to the contestant who has performed a technique that is not completely decisive.*

YAMAE (YAME) – Finish, halt, stop, recover, return. *Used by instructors to halt or stop training. Also used by the referee in Kumite competition to interrupt or end a match as he chops down with his hands and the time keeper stops the clock.*

ZOKKO – Start again, attack, fight. *A command given by the referee for competitors to restart the bout or to urge competitors to attack/fight.*

ZU ZUKI (ZU TSUKI) – Head thrust. *This is not permitted in completion and is considered a foul (Hansoku).*

16

Martial Arts
(Budo)

This section contains general terminology used
in Karate-Do and martial arts in general
including names of influential individuals and
styles of martial arts.

武
道

AI – Harmony. *Blending, harmony in movement.*

AIKI – Harmony spirit, united spirit. *The spiritual principle of overcoming an adversary (externally or internally) by harmonizing with his force and re–directing it.*

AIKIDO – The way of harmony, flowing harmony way. *Martial art believed to have originated as AIKIJUJTSU near the year 1100. The art of Aikido as we know it today was founded by Morihei Ueshiba (1883–1970). It is said that Ueshiba learned the basics of Aikijujutsu from Sokaku Takeda (the seventh generation of the Takeda family), and in a moment of spiritual enlightenment, or Satori, envisioned aikido.*

AIKIJUJUTSU – Flowing harmony art. *Martial art that is historically regarded as the root, or birth, of DAITO RYU, and all classical systems of jujutsu, including aikido.*

ANTIE – Balance, equilibrium.

ASA GEIKO – Morning Training in the summer.

AU – To meet. *As, in to meet an opponent in contest.*

AZATO - Yasutsune "Ankoh" Azato (1828-1906). *Master of Okinawa Karate, son of a Tonichi, one of the two highest classes of the Okinawan society, the was born in the town of Azato. He was the advisor to the Okinawan King and an expert in horseriding, kendo and archery. One the two most important teachers of Master Gichin Funakoshi.*

BATTOJUTSU – Sword cutting technique.

BO – Wooden staff used as a weapon. *Made of oak wood approximately 6 feet (180 cm long).*

BOGU – Protective equipment, body armour.

BOGU KUMITE – Fighting with protective equipment.

BO JUTSU – Wooden staff art, art of the wooden staff.

142

BOKEN – Wooden sword.

BO SAI KUMITE – Sparring with a staff and short weapon with two prongs.

BO–UCHI – Bo strike. *A general term for any strike using a Bo.*

BO UKE – Blocking stick. *A general term for all blocks against a Bo.*

BU – Military.

BUDO – **Martial arts way, way of the *warrior*. *Originally referring to a warrior's way of life devoted to self–development. Now, more commonly used in reference to particular combative systems The Japanese character for BU (martial or military) is derived from characters meaning "Stop" and (a weapon like a) "Halberd". In conjunction, then, BU may have the connotation "to stop the halberd."***

BUDOKA – Student of the martial, student of military arts.

BUGEI – Martial arts. *The Classical methods of fighting as developed by Japanese warriors (Samurai) for the sole purpose of real combat.*

BUGEI SHA – Martial arts person.

BUJUTSU – Martial art techniques, military arts techniques. *The Classical methods of fighting as developed by Japanese warriors (Samurai).*

BUKE – Person of military class or samurai.

BUKI HO – Weapons training.

BUSHI – Warrior. *The Samurai class, stressing the importance of loyalty, bravery, integrity, respect and honour.*

BUSHI NO TE (BUSHI TE) – Warrior's hands.

143

BUSHI DO – Way of the warrior. *The martial ethic developed among warriors in Japan's medieval and feudal periods. Derived from the practical ethics held in common by the Samurai class, stressing the importance of loyalty, bravery, integrity, respect and honour.*

BUSHI KAI – Warrior's society.

BUTOKUKAN – Martial values.

BYOBUDAOSHI – To topple a folding screen. *Throwing technique where the leg is placed behind the attacker's front leg and swept while simultaneous pushing his chin and head back with an open hand in the opposite direction as leg being swept.*

CHAKUGAN – Focus and attention.

CHI – Spirit, air, breath, vital energy, life force.

CHIBANA – Chosin Chibana (1885 – 1969). He was born at Tottori Cho in Shuri City, Okinawa. *He began his Karate training with Yasutsune "Ankoh" Itosu in 1900 with whom he studied until Itosu's death in 1915.*

CHIKARAISHI – Power stone. *Okinawan training device.*

CHIKARA KURABE – Early Japanese fighting system.

CHISHI – Stone lever used to develop power. *Used by Goju–Ryu karateka.*

CHITO RYU – Karate style founded by Dr.Tsuyoshi Chitose. *It emphasizes conditioning of the mind and body before the actual practice of self defence. A combination of Goju–Ryu and Shorin–Ryu.*

CHOJUN MIYAGI – Chojun Miyagi (Miagi) (1888–1952). *See Miyai.*

CHOKI MOTOBU - Choki Motobu (1871-1944). *See Motobu.*

CHOSIN CHIBANA – Chosin Chibana (1885 – 1969). *See Chibana.*

CHOTOKU KYAN – Chotoku Kyan (1869–1945). *See Kyan.*

CHOMO HANASHIRO – Chomo Hanashiro (1867–1944). *See Hanashiro.*

CHOWASURU – To harmonise with an opponent.

CHOU MOTOBU – Chou Motobu (1870–1944). *See Motobu.*

CHOYU MOTOBU – Choyu Motobu (1867–1930). *See Motobu.*

CHU'AN FA – Way of the fist (Kempo in Japanese).

CHUDAN – Middle level, chest, mid–section. *From the waist to the shoulders. Typically aimed at the solar plexus.*

DAI NIPPON BUTOKUKAI – Great Japan Martial Virtues Association.

DAISHO – The term given to the two swords customarily worn by Samurai.

DAITO   The long sword with curved blade. *Also known as Katana. When worn in combination with the short sword in identical scabbards or Koshirae, the set would be referred to as Daisho. The Daisho or Daito could only be worn by samurai of higher rank.*

DAITO RYU – Great Eastern School. *A school of classical martial arts dating from the Heian period and passed down through the Takeda family.*

DAN (DANI) – Level, rank or degree. *Black belt rank.*

DEMURA - Fumio Demura (1938--). He was born in Yokohama, Japan in 1938. *He started practicing karate at the age of 8 and* *started studying Kendo and Karate under Ryusho Sakagami at the age of 12.*

DO – Way, path of life. *The Japanese character for "DO" is the same as the Chinese character for Tao (as in "Taoism"). In Karate, the connotation is that of a way of attaining spiritual enlightenment or a way of improving one's character through traditional training. Also means 'torso', 'truck of the body', 'movement', 'activity'.*

DOGI – Martial arts uniform. *Also referred to as Gi or Karate Gi.*

DOGU – Tools, equipment, instruments. *General term for equipment used in martial arts practice.*

DOJI WAZA – Simultaneous techniques. *When opponents perform a technique at the same time.*

DOJO – Place of the way, training hall. *Also "place of enlightenment." The place where Karate is practiced or traditional martial arts training hall.*

DOJO KUN – Code of the dojo. School Principles, Rules.

DOKAN – The ring of the way; repetition, constant practice.

DORI – Practice.

EGAMI - Shigeru Egami (1912-1981). Master Shigeru Egami was born in the Fukuoka Prefecture in 1912. *He was one of Gichin Funakoshi earliest students, but more than this, he was one of his most faithful and correct followers. Egami met Master Funakoshi when he was 18 years old when he began studying at Waseda University. Before this he had already practiced Judo, Kendo and Aikido.*

EKKUA (EKKU) – Improvised weapon made from fisherman's oar. *Use as a staff or spear by the Okinawa's.*

ENOEDA - Keinosuke Enoeda (1953-2003). He was born in the city of Fukouka, Kyushu, Japan in 1935. *On entering Takushohu university in Tokyo in 1953 he studied martial arts and was trained by Master Gichin Funakoshi and late Master Masatoshi Nakayama, 10th Dan and the former Chief Instructor of the Japan Karate Association.*

ERI – Lapel of the Gi.

FUKAI – To hold strongly.

FUKYU – Fundamental, basic.

FUMIO DEMURA - Fumio Demura (1938--). *See Demura.*

FUNAKOSHI – Gichin Funakoshi (1868–1957). See Gichin.

FUNAKOSHI – Yoshitaka Gigo Funakoshi (1906 - 1945). The third son of Gichin Funakoshi and the creator of Modern Japanese Karate-do technique. *Whereas his father was responsible for transforming karate from a fighting technique to a philosophical martial do (way of life), Yoshitaka with the support of his farther and other important martial artists was responsible for developing karate technique. Yoshitaka began his formal training in karate when he was 12 years of age, but much before that he had been in contact with karate.*

GASSHUKUA – Special training camp at Japanese universities.

GETA – Wooden or iron clogs used to strengthen feet.

GI – **Jacket, uniform, suit.** *A training costume consisting of pants and a loose jacket tied with a belt and is most often white in colour. Also referred to as Do–Gi or Karate–Gi, the term given to uniform worn by practitioners of traditional Japanese martial arts.*

GICHIN FUNAKOSHI – Gichin Funakoshi (1868–1957). *Called the father of Japanese Karate and founded Shotokan, one of the most popular styles of Karate in the world today. Born in Shuri, he began his Karate training under Yasutsune Asato and* *later Yasutsune Itosu, both students of the great Sokon "Bushi" Matsumura. Funakoshi himself also occasionally trained with Matsumura.*

GOJU RYU – Hard/Soft Way. *Traditional karate style founded by Chojun Myaghi. This is a traditional concept of universal balance as in the Chinese "Yin–Yang" and the Japanese "In–Yo".*

GOSHIN – Self defence.

GOSHIN BUDO – Defence martial arts.

GOSHIN JUTSU – Art of self defence.

HAKAMA – Divided skirt. *Pleated, skirt–like pants worn by practitioners of classical Japanese martial arts.*

HAKKO RYU – Eighth–light School. *A jujutsu system developed from Daito Ryu Jujutsu by Ryuho Okuyama in 1941.*

HAKUTSURU – White crane/stork techniques in Okinawan karate.

HANASHIRO – Chomo Hanashiro (1867–1944). *Shorin Ryu master. He was a classmate of Kentsu Yabu, Gichin Funakoshi, and Chotoku Kyan under Bushi Matsumura and Yasutsune Itosu.*

HAPPO KUMITE – Defence against eight opponents grouped in a circle.

HARAGEI – Stomach Arts. *Developing Ki (chi) energy.*

HENKA WAZA – Changing techniques. *Techniques used after Oyo Waza is applied. Henka Waza is varied and mainly, dependent on the given condition. Toes and heels together.*

HIGA – Machu Higa (1790–1870). *He served as a bodyguard for the Ryukyuan royal family for which and was awarded the* *title Peichin, signifying membership in the Okinawan Shizoku which was equivalent to the Japanese Samurai class.*

HIGASHIONNA – Kanryo Higashionna (1851–1915). *He was good friend of Yasutsune Itosu and he was regarded as one of the most influential Karate instructors in Okinawan history. As a leading developer and master of Naha Te, he laid the foundation for Goju Ryu which was subsequently formalized by his senior student, Chojun Miyagi.*

HIRONORI OHTSUKA - Hironori Ohtsuka (1892 - 1982). *See Ohtsuka.*

HISHIRYO – Think without thinking, consciousness beyond thought.

HO – Rules.

HOMBU (HONBU) – **Central dojo, headquarters.** *A term used to refer to the martial arts headquarters of an organization.*

HOMBU DOJO – **Head training hall.** *The central most senior dojo of an organisation.*

HYOTEKI – Cable, target. *Using belt to aid focus of technique.*

IAI – Swordplay.

IAIDO – Way of the sword, way of samurai sword draw.

IBUKI – Breath control, controlled breathing, method of breathing.

ICHIBYOSHI – In one breath. *To take advantage of the ideal striking distance in kumite and quickly striking "in one breath" without making any preliminary movement.*

IKKEN HISSATSU – Kill with one blow.

INIBUKI – Passive internal breathing.

IRO OBI – Coloured belt.

ISSHIN RYU –   One heart school. *Okinawan style of Karate combining the elements of Shorin–Ryu and Goju–Ryu. Founded by Tatsuo Shimabuku, in 1954.*

ITOSU – Yasutsune "Ankoh" Itosu (1830–1915). *He was born in the city of Shuri, Okinawa. At the age of 16 he started to train in Karate with Master Sokon "Bushi" Matsumura. He simplified many of the ancient katas, created several new ones of his own, and pioneered teaching methods that would revolutionize the art by making its study easier and less dangerous for future generations. One the two most important teachers of Master Gichin Funakoshi.*

ITTO TENSHIN RYU – A school of Kenjutsu (Art of the Sword) from the Edo period, founded by Kurosawa Kojiro, legendary foe of Miyamoto Musashi.

JIAI – Affection, love kindness. *Meaning one is in harmony with one's self and those he meets. Said to have been the salutations used by the monks of the temple of Ji–on.*

JO – Wooden staff about 4–5 feet (120–150 cm) in length and 2 inches (5 cm) thick. *The Jo originated as a walking stick.*

JO DO – Way of the 4 foot staff.

JO HINERI – Jo twist. *As performed in the Kata Bassai Sho.*

JUJUSTU (JUJITSU) – Art of gentleness. *Ju Jitsu is a martial art based on joint locks and throwing techniques that disarm and control an attacker.*

JOKYU   RENRAKU   WAZA – Advanced   combination techniques.

JOSEKI – Upper side of dojo.

JO TSUKAMI WAZA – Jo grasping techniques.

JUDO – Yielding way, gentle way, the way of gentleness. *Contemporary Budo style and sport derived from JUJUTSU and founded by Jigoro Kano in 1881.*

JUTSU – Art. *Art of combat application.*

JUTTE – Forked iron truncheon.

KA – Person or practitioner.

KAGI YARI – Essential spear.

KAI – Style.

KAIKEN – Short knife.

KAKE WAZA – Hooking techniques.

KAKUSHI WAZA (KAKUSHIN WAZA) – Hidden techniques.

KAMA – Reaping sickle. *This is an Okinawan farming implement used as a weapon.*

KAMA YARI – Sickle spear.

KAMIZA – *Spirit seat,* divine or upper seat in dojo. *A holy place, or shelf on the front wall of traditional Japanese dojos, where a shrine often resides.*

KANAZAWA – Hirokazu Kanazawa(1931 –). *Student of and successor to Master Gichin Funakoshi. He was born in Iwate Prefecture, Japan on May 3, 1931. He attended Tokushaku University where he studied the Shotokan Karate under Okazaki, Masatoshi Nakayama (1913-1987), Hidetaka Nishiyama (1928), and other senior instructors. Upon graduation in 1956, he joined the Japan Karate Association ("JKA") and became one of the first candidates to complete its instructor's course.*

151

KANGEIKO – Cold practise.

KANRYO HIGASHIONNA – Kanryo Higashionna (1851–1915). *See Higashionna.*

KANZUI – Approval of wood breaking. *Judges confirmation.*

KAPPO – Techniques of resuscitating people who have succumbed to a shock to the nervous system.

KARATE – Empty hand, empty hand fighting. *When Karate was first introduced to Japan, it was called To–De which means 'Chinese hand'.*

KARATEKA – Student of Karate.

KARATE DO – Empty hand way, the way of the empty hand. *Martial art developed on the island of Okinawa. The name implies not only the physical aspect of Karate, but the mental and social aspects also.*

KARATEKA – A practitioner/student of karate.

KARATE JUTSU – Empty hand art. *System of unarmed combat developed on the island of Okinawa.*

KARATE NI SENTENASHI – In Karate there is no first strike. *A phrase used to state the essence of Karate Do.*

KARATE DO NYUMON – A passage through the gates of the Karate way. *The first book written by Gichin Funakoshi.*

KASE – Master Taiji Kase (1929-2004). Born in 09th February 1929 in Tokyo. *Student of Gichin Funakoshi and his son Yoshitaka Funakoshi. Later he was a student of Sensei Okujama.*

KATANA – The long sword with curved blade. *Also known as Daito. When worn in combination with the short sword in identical scabbards or Koshirae, the set would be referred to as*

Daisho. The Daisho or Daito could only be worn by samurai of higher rank.

KATAWAGURUMA – Half wheel. *Throwing technique.*

KATSU (KUATSU):
(1) – Resuscitating method. *Method for resuscitating one who has lost consciousness due to strangulation or shock.*
(2) – Victory, to win.
(3) – Type of loud shout. *Similar to Kiai.*

KEIBO – Wooden club.

KEIKO – Training, practice, drill. *The only secret to success in Karate. Also means 'joined fingertips', 'chicken beak hand'.*

KEMPO – Way of the fist, fist law. *A generic term to describe fighting systems that uses the fist.*

KEN – Fist, closed hand technique, sword. *Also means 'tendon', 'active condition' and 'alert state'.*

KENDO – The way of the sword. – *Fencing method developed from Kenjutsu (art of the sword).* Its origins are in Japan's samurai culture and swordsmanship Heavily protected fighters spar offensively with wooden swords.

KEN JUTSU – Art of the sword. The art of *classical Japanese* combative swordsmanship.

KENPO – Martial art that employs linear as well as circular techniques, using intermittent power when and where needed, interspersed with major and minor moves that flow with encounters as they occur.

KENSEI – The technique with silent Kiai. Related to meditation.

KENTSU – Yabu Kentsu (1865–1945). *A prominent Shorin Ryu master who was known for his fighting ability. It is said that he never lost a fight, beating even the great Choki Motobu in a* *famous challenge match. Yabu began his Karate training under Sokon "Bushi" Matsumura and later continued under Matsumura's top student, Yasutsune Itosu.*

KENWA MABUNI – Kenwa Mabuni (1890–1952). *See Mabuni.*

KI – Mind. Spirit, energy, vital–force, channelled life force. *The term used to describe the life force present and flowing in all living things. The Chinese refer to this as chi.*

KIAI – Harmonious energy, spirited shout, expression of spirit. *A shout delivered for the purpose of focusing all of one's energy into a single movement. Expression of vital spirit. Even when audible Kiai are absent, one should try to preserve the feeling of Kiai at certain crucial points within karate techniques. Manifestation of Ki is the simultaneous union of spirit and expression of physical strength.*

KIAI JUTSU – Art of spirit meeting, expressing life force.

KI KEN TAI NO ITCHI – Spirit, technique and body as one.

KIHAKU – Spirit.

KIHON – **Basic techniques.**

KIME – **Focusing the muscles, tension.**

KIMETE – Deciding blow. *The strike that decides the winner.*

KIME WAZA – Decisive techniques.

KIMOCHI – Attitude.

KOBAYASHI RYU – Small forest. *An Okinawam form of Shorin Ryu karate.*

KO BO ICHI – The concept of attack–defence connection.

KOBUDO – Weapons way, ancient martial arts ways.

KOBU JUTSU – Art of ancient weapons.

KOEI KAN – **Japanese style of karate founded by Eizo Onishi in 1952.** *In Koei–Kan the individual is stressed, and each student is taught to strive for the highest degree of self–attainment.*

KOKEGI – Attacker.

KOKEN – Bent wrist, wrist joint.

KOKO KIZA KUZUSHI – Tiger mouth knee take down. *As performed in the Kata Nijushiho.*

KOKORO – Spirit, heart, mind, feeling. *In Japanese culture, the spirit dwells in the heart.*

KOKUBA - Kosei Kokuba (1901 - 1959). He was was born in Naha City, Okinawa in 1901 the youngest son of a samurai family descended from the Sho-Shi royal family of Okinawa. *The father of Shogo Kuniba and the founder of Motobu-ha Shito-ryu.*

KOKYU – Breathing rhythm.

KOMANAGE – Spinning top. *Throwing technique.*

KOROSIII WAZA – Killing techniques.

KOSAKU MATSUMORA – Kosaku Matsumora (1828–1898). *See Matsumora.*

KOSEI KOKUBA - Kosei Kokuba (1901 - 1959). *See Kokuba.*

KOSHIRAE – The short sword. *When worn in combination with the long curved sword in identical scabbards or Daito, the set would be referred to as Daisho. The Daisho could only be worn by samurai of higher rank.*

KOSHI WAZA – **Hip techniques.**

KUATSU – *See Katsu.*

155

KUBIWA – To encircle the neck. *Throwing technique.*

KUJI KIRI – Energy channelling.

KUMADE – Bear hand. *Fingers and thumb are bent to touch the palm of the hand in a claw like fashion. Used mainly for attacking the ears and face. Also means 'rake', 'fork'.*

KUNG FU – Skill, time, strength, ability, task, work. Chinese martial art.

KUNIBA - Shogo Kuniba (1935 -). Son of master Kosei Kuniba was born on February 5, 1935 in Yamanashi prefecture near Mt. Fuji in the city of Fuji-Yoshida-Shi.

KUSANKU – Chinese military attaché who created the forerunner to the Kata Kanku Dai.

KUSARIGAMA – Japanese version of kama. Reaping sickle with chain.

KUZUSHI – Leverage. *Crushing the enemy.*

KWANKU – Okinawan pronunciation of Kanku.

KYAN – Chotoku Kyan (1869–1945). *A legendary master even during his own lifetime. He was an important teacher who fathered a long line of Shorin Ryu styles.*

KYOKUSHINKAI – School of ultimate truth. *Style of karate founded from Goju Ryu and Shotokan by Master Matsutatsu Oyama.*

KYUBA NO MICHI DO – The way of the bow and horse. *A code of warrior ethics developed in the 12th century during the reign of Minamoto Yoritomo, also known as Kyusen No Michi Do (the way of the bow and arrow).*

KYUDO – The way of the bow. *The classical art of Japanese archery.*

156

KYU JUTSU – The art of the bow. *The art of combative archery.*

KYUSHO – Vital points.

KYUSHO WAZA – Pressure point techniques.

KYUSHU JUTSU – The art of striking vital points.

MABUNI – Kenwa Mabuni (1887–1952). *Among the first Okinawan masters to teach on mainland Japan. He was a student of both Yasutsune "Anko" Itosu & Kanryu Higashionna and the founded Shito Ryu, one of the four main styles of Karate studied in Japan today.*

MACHI DOJO – Small training hall.

MACHU HIGA – Machu Higa (1790–1870). *See Higa.*

MAE UKEMI – Forward fall/roll.

MAKIWARA – Wooden striking post, punching board. Traditionally covered with straw.

MAKOTO – A feeling of complete sincerity. *This requires an honest, pure mind, free from external pressure.*

MANABU – Learning by imitating. *A method of studying and copying the movements and techniques demonstrated by the instructor.*

MATSUMORA – Kosaku Matsumora (1828–1898). *He was a leading practitioner, developer, and teacher of Tomari–Te, the Karate that developed around Tomari village. Although Tomari–Te has not survived as a distinct system, many of its katas and techniques are incorporated within the Shorin–Ryu styles of today.*

MATSUMURA – Sokon "Bushi" Matsumura (1798–1890). *The father of Okinawan Karate, Sokon "Bushi" (Warrior)*

Matsumura was the first to systemize Shuri–Te from which the various Shorin–Ryu styles have come down to us today.

MIKAMI - Takayuki Mikami. Born in Niigata, Japan in 1933. *JKA 8th Dan instructor and the chief instructor of ASKF based in Metairie, Louisiana USA (southern region of the International Shotokan Karate Federation) which he founded in 1965.*

MIYAGI – Chojun Miyagi (1888–1952). *A Karate pioneer and innovator. He built upon the Naha Te of his teacher, Kanryo Higashionna, to develop his own style which he called Goju Ryu.*

MIZU NO KOKORO – Mind like water. *A psychological principle emphasising the state of mind required while facing an opponent.*

MOKUSO – Deep breathing and empty mind.

MOROTE JO DORI – Double handed Jo staff catch, augmented Jo grab. *As performed in the Kata Jitte.*

MOROTE JO UKE – Double handed Jo staff block. *As performed in the Kata Meikyo.*

MOTOBU - Choki Motobu (1871-1944). He was born in 1871 in the village of Akahira in the Shuri region of Okinawa. *Choki was the third son of Udun Motobu a high ranking Aji (lord).*

MOTOBU – Chou Motobu (1870–1944). *He is perhaps the most controversial of all the great Karate masters. He first gained notoriety as a bully and a braggart. In later life he adopted a more humble attitude but was never able to outlive his earlier reputation.*

MOTOBU – Choyu Motobu (1867–1930). *He was the first–born son of a ranking lord and a descendent of the Ryukyuan King Sho Shitsu (reigned 1648–1669), was trained in Go–Ten–Te (palace hand), the secret martial art of the royal family which had been handed down within the Motobu family from father to first–born son for eleven generations.*

158

MUNEN MUSO – Free of all ideas and thoughts. *This is in preparation for combat or Kata.*

MUSHIN – No Mind. *The term used to describe the state of pure consciousness unburdened by thought and being free and flexible to react and adapt to a given situation.*

NABE MATSUMURA – Nabe Matsumura (1850–1943*). He was a prominent Karate master of his time and the grandson of the great Sokon Matsumura. He became successor to the family system when Sokon died thereby serving as a link between the old masters and those of the present day.*

NAGE WAZA – Throwing techniques.

NAGINATA – Japanese weapon consisting of a blade mounted on a long staff.

NAGORE (NOGARE) – Deep breathing, correct breath control. Method of breathing used in Kata.

NAHA TE – Naha hand. *Early Okinawan karate style.*

NAKAMURA – Shigeru Nakamura (1892–1969). *Founder of Okinawa Kempo. He was a living legend and one of Okinawa's all time great Karate masters.*

NAKAYAMA – Matoshi Nakayama (1913-198/). Born in Kanazawa, Japan. *His family was of a line of samurai and kendo instructorsand his father, Naotoshi, also studied judo and was a doctor in the army. As a young boy his family re-settled in Taipei, Taiwan where Masatoshi Nakayama began his primary school education. In addition to his academic studies, he was dedicated to kendo, judo, swimming, skiing, tennis and athletics.*

NINJA – Stealer, spy. *Allegedly possessing extraordinary martial abilities.*

159

NINJUTSU – The art of steeling. *One of the most mysterious arts of feudal Japan and espionage system. Cloaked in secrecy, the original ninjitsu practitioners were the terrorists of their era. They were families of spies and assassins hired by Japanese warlords to infiltrate and terrorize enemies.*

NISHIYAMA - Master Hidetaka Nishiyama considered to be one of the great masters and pioneers of Japanese Traditional Karate. *He began his study in 1943 at the age of fifteen, with Master Gichin Funakoshi. He was one of the original founders of the Japan Karate Association, which has produced some of the most famous karate masters in the world: Kanazawa, Enoeda, Shirai and Mikami.*

NUKETE IRU – Out of target.

NUNCHAKU – Wooden rice flail. *An Okinawan weapon consisting of two sticks connected by rope or chain. This was originally used by the Okinawa's as a farm tool to thrash rice straw.*

OBI (OBE) – A belt.

ODACHI – Great sword.

OHTSUKA - Hironori Ohtsuka (1892 - 1982). He was born on 1st June 1892 in Shimodate City, Ibaraki Prefecture, Japan. *A Student of Gichin Funakoshi and was the founder of the Wado-ryu style during the 1920s and 1930s.*

OKINAWA TE – Okinawa hand. *Empty hand martial art of the Ryukyu Islands.*

OKUDEN – Hidden teachings. *Sometimes referred to as, Okuden Waza.*

ONAJI WAZA – Same technique.

REI – Zero. *Also mean bow, the sign of respect.*

160

REIGI (REIGISAHO) – Etiquette, formal dojo customs. The correct behaviour or manors to be observed. This is particularly relevant in the Dojo. Respect of others in the Dojo and discipline are essential factors to be employed at all time. To observe the etiquette is to demonstrate one's willingness to learn, to pay attention and take part in the training and practice of techniques. Also referred to as Reishiki

REISHIKI – Etiquette. *See Reigi.*

RENMEI – League, union, alliance.

RENRAKU WAZA – Combination techniques. *Also referred to as Renzoku Waza.*

RENSEI – Practice tournament. Competitors receive advise on their performances.

RENSHU – Practice, training period. *To study.*

RENZOKU WAZA – Combination techniques. *Also referred to as Renraku Waza.*

RITSUREI – Standing bow.

ROKUSHAKUBO – Six foot staff.

RONIN – A leaderless samurai. *Generally considered to be of low moral virtue.*

RYU:
(1) – Way, school, system, style, method. Usually used in reference to particular schools or styles of classical martial arts e.g. Shotokan–Ryu, Wado–Ryu, Goju–Ryu, Shito–Ryu etc.
(2) – Double.
(3) – Dragon.

RYUSHO SAKAGAMI - Ryusho Sakagami (1915-1993). *See Sakagami.*

SAHO – Etiquette.

SAI – Weapon which looks like a Trident. *An Okinawan weapon used in close combat and is shaped like the Greek letter Psi with the middle being much longer.*

SAKAGAMI - Ryusho Sakagami (1915-1993). He was born in Hyogo Prefecture, Kawanishi City of Japan, the son of a very prosperous "Saki" (rice wine) family businessman. *He began practicing the martial art of 'Kendo" around the age of ten and in his later teen years began to study "Iaido".*

SAKATSUCHI – To hammer upside down. *Throwing technique.*

SAKUGAWA – Satunushi Tode Sakugawa (1762–1843). *Recognized as one of the most important figures in the history of Karate. He was among the first to blend elements of the original Okinawan art of Te with Chinese boxing (Tode).*

SAMURAI – One who serves, warrior. *From the verb, "Saburau", meaning to serve. A member of the elite class of warriors in feudal Japan's social order.*

SANDA KINJO – Sanda Kinjo "Ufuchiku" (1841–1926). *Born in Shuri, he was a pioneering Karate and Kobudo expert who served as personal bodyguard to the last of Okinawa's reigning king's, Sho Tai, until the king's fall from power in 1879.*

SAPPO – Method of causing serious injury or death by attacking vital points.

SATORI – Enlightenment, spiritual enlightenment.

SEI – Tranquility, inactivity.

SEIDOKAN – Okinawan Karate system founded by Soke Toma. *It combines the punching, kicking and blocking techniques of Karate, the throwing and joint locking techniques of Aiki–Ju–Jutsu and traditional Okinawian weaponry.*

SEIRYOKU ZEN YO KOKUMIN TAIIKU NO KATA – Method of building ones physical education form.

SEISAN (SEISHAN) – Okinawan Kata. *An older version of the Kata Hangetsu.*

SEISHAN DACHI (TATTE SEISHAN DACHI) – Hourglass stance.

SEISHIN – Mind, soul, spirit.

SEMETE – Attacker.

SENI – Fighting will, spirit.

SHAO LIN – Kung Fu method based on eight postures and five animal forms. *Also means 'small forest'.*

SHIGERU NAKAMURA – Shigeru Nakamura (1892–1969). *See Nakamura.*

SHIHO WARI – Breaking boards in four directions to test one's strength.

SHIMABUKU – Tatsuo Shimabuku (1908–1975). *An important innovator. He developed Isshin Ryu to correct what he felt were deficiencies in the Karate styles he had studied.*

SHIMABUKURO – Zenryo Shimabukuro (1909–1969). *He strived to preserve the classic Karate of Chotoku Kyan and, in so doing, became one of the most respected masters of modern times.*

SHIMODE - Takeshi Shimoda Sensei (1901-1934). *A devoted and talented student of Gichin Funakoshi he accompanied Gichin and Yoshitaka on their travels to Japan to give demonstrations and lectures on the martial arts. He was an expert in Kendo and also a student of Ninjutsu.*

SHIMOSEKI – Lower seat in dojo.

163

SHIPMAN (SHINPAN) – Referee.

SHINKYU SHIAI – Method of examination/grading for Kyu grades.

SHINSHIN – Stopped mind.

SHIPPAI – Failure to break wood. *Judges decision.*

SHIRAI – Master Hiroshi Shirai. Born 1937. JKA instructor and head of World Shotokan Institute. *Trained at the Komazawa University under Sensei Nishiyama and sensei Tsujima.*

SHIRO OBI – White belt.

SHITO RYU – Okinawan style of Karate founded by Kenwa Mabuni. Predominately a hard style that embraces Kata from the hard Shorin–Ryu and the softer Goju–Ryu styles.

SHOBU ZUYOSA – Snatching victory from the jaws of defeat.

SHOGO KUNIBA - Shogo Kuniba (1935 -). *See Kuniba.*

SHOMEI – Front central area of the dojo. *Also referred to as Shomen.*

SHOREI RYU – Okinawan style of Karate. *Based on hard and heavy physical movements and on five major animal strengths such as, the dragon (body strength), the tiger (bone strength), the leopard (inner and outer strength), the snake (breath strength), and the crane (spiritual strength).*

SHORINJI KEMPO – Shorinji fist way.

SHORIN RYU – Okinawan style of Karate. *Based on light and fast movements and more upright stances than most Japanese styles of karate.*

SHOSHINSHA – Beginner, novice.

164

SHOTO – Pine waves, waving pines, a breeze through the pines. *Gichin Funakoshi's pen name.*

SHOTOKAN – Shoto's house, house of Shoto. *The Shotokan style of Karate founded by Gichin Funakoshi. Gichin Funakoshi practised calligraphy and wrote and published his books of poetry, signing his work with his pen name Shoto. Hence his dojo in Tokyo (and style) became known as Shoto's House or Shotokan. The first historically recognized school of Karate, as founded by Gichin Funakoshi in 1922.*

SHUBO – Stick arm, arm stick.

SHUCHU SURU – Total concentration.

SHUGORO NAKAZATO – Shugoro Nakazato. *He was born in Nahn–city Okinawa in 1919. While attending normal school in Osaka Japan in 1935, he began his study of Karate at the age of 16 under the instruction of Ishu Selichl. Nakazato studied under Sensei Ishu for 6 years. During the war, he was in the Japanese Calvary.*

SHUGYO – Rigorous training, austere practice.

SHUGYOSHA – One who is intense in training.

SHUMATSU UNDO – Warm down exercises at the end of a training session/lesson.

SHURI TE – Shuri hand. *One of three main types of karate in Okinawa.*

SOKON MATSUMURA – Sokon "Bushi" Matsumura (1798–1890). *See Matsumura.*

SUN DOME – Control. To arrest a technique just before contact with the target.

SUTEMI – Sacrifice.

165

SUTEMI WAZA – Last chance technique.

TACHI:
(1) – A Japanese long sword.
(2) – Standing stance.

TAE KWON DO – Korean martial art. *Meaning the way of punching and kicking.*

TAI – State of reserve, inactive condition.

TAI CHI CH'UAN – Chinese martial art used to improve health. *Meaning grand ultimate fist.*

TAMBO – Short stick.

TAMESHI WARA (TAMESHI WARI) – Trial by wood, breaking. Test of strength by the breaking of materials using various bare handed techniques.

TANIOTOSHI – To push off a cliff. *Throwing technique.*

TASHI – Expert in Japanese martial arts. *Usually third or fourth Dan.*

TATAMI – Straw floor mat. *Traditionally a straw mat used to protect from falling. Approximately 3 x 6 feet (1m x 1.8m) in size and 3 inches (8 cm) thick. Now days these are usually made of bound straw and covered in vinyl.*

TATE FUSE – Taking cover, going to ground.

TATSUO SHIMABUKU – Tatsuo Shimabuku (1908–1975). *See Shimabuku.*

TE – Hand. *Historically regarded as the name originally given to the system of empty handed combat system as developed on Okinawa.*

TEKKAN ZU – Metal rings used to strike vital points.

166

TEKKI – Spiked metal knuckledusters. Also a series of 3 Kata of Chinese origin translated as "Iron Horse" or "Horse riding". Originally a single Kata named Naihanchi.

TESSEN – Metal fan used as a weapon.

TE WAZA – Hand techniques.

TO DE – An old Okinawan name for Karate, also see Okinawa–Te and To–Te.

TODE SAKUGAWA – Satunushi Tode Sakugawa (1762–1843). *See   Sakugawa..*

TO TE – T'ang hand. Introduced into Okinawa around 1372.

TOMARI TE – Tomari hand.

TONFA – Handle. *Farming implement developed into a weapon by the Okinawans.*

TONFA (TOIFA) – Millstone handle.

TONFA JUTSU – Combative use of the millstone handle.

TORI – Hold the attacker.

TOSHI – Fighting spirit.

TSUBAMEGAESHI – V turning swallow. *Throwing technique.*

TSUKI NO KOKORO (ZUKI NO KOKORO) – A mind like the moon.

TSUKI TE (ZUKI TE) – Hand attacks, to fight.

TSUKKOMI – Charging.

TSUYOKI – Strong sprit.

TSUYOKU – Strongly.

167

UECHI RYU – Okinawan style of karate founded by Kanbon Uechi.

UNDOO – Callisthenics performed before karate training.

WA – Accord, peace, harmony. *The classical concept of non–resistance.*

WADO RYU – Way of peace and harmony school. *One of the four major Japanese Karate styles founded in 1939 by Hironori Ohtsuka who was a former student of Ginchin Funakoshi. The style is a combination of Shotokan and Yoshin Ryu Jujutsu.*

WADO KAI – Association of pupil of the way of peace and harmony.

WADOKAN – Club house of the way of peace and harmony.

WAKIZASHI – The short samurai sword, also known as Shoto. *This could be worn by merchants, tradesmen and craftsmen, unlike the long sword. The short sword and long sword worn in combination and mounted in identical scabbards or Koshirae are referred to as Daisho and could only be worn by higher ranking samurai.*

WAZA – **Technique(s).**

WAZA O HODOKOSU KOKI – Psychological moment to execute technique.

WING CHUN – Beautiful springtime. *A form of Kung Fu based on linear punches named after a nun of the Shako–Lin temple.*

WUTANG – School of Kung Fu.

YABU KENTSU – Yabu Kentsu (1865–1945). *See Kentsu.*

YABUSAME – Mounted archery.

YANG – Active, positive.

YARI – Spear.

YARIDAMA – To spear a ball. *Throwing technique.*

YASUTUNE AZATO - Yasutsune "Ankoh" Azato (1828-1906). *See Azato.*

YASUTSUNE ITOSU – Yasutsune "Ankoh" Itosu (1830–1915). *See Itosu.*

YAWARA – Gentle, soft, control. *Ancient method of Japanese unarmed combat.*

YIN – Passive, negative.

YOWAI – Weak focus.

YUBIJUTSU – Art of using one's finger to attack vital point on the body.

YUMI – Bow, as in archery.

ZANSHIN – **Remaining mind or heart.** *Awareness of one's surroundings. Even after a technique has been completed, one should remain in a balanced and aware state.*

ZA ZEN – Zen meditation.

ZEN – **Buddhist sect, religious meditation.** *One of the major branches of Mahayana Buddhism that arose in China and flourished following its introduction there in the 13th century. Japanese method of enlightenment based on the teachings Buddhism which are traditionally linked to Karate.*

ZENRYO SHIMABUKURO – Zenryo Shimabukuro (1909–1969). *See Shimabukro.*

ZUKI NO KOKORO (TSUKI NO KOKORO) – A mind like the moon.

ZUKI TE (TSUKI TE) – Hand Attacks.

170

17

Commands & Communication (Gorei To Reigi)

This section contains terminology, phrases, commands, instruction, announcements and other communications made in the dojo or in competitive events.

号令と礼儀

ANA TA NO KACHI – You are the winner.

ANA TA WA – And you?

ARIGATO GOZAIMASU (ARIGATO) – Thank you.

ATO DE – Later.

AWASE – Combined.

CHUDAN – **Middle area of body, chest and stomach.** *When engaging in Kihon Kumite the attacker will announce his intended target area before executing the attack. This allows the defender the opportunity to prepare for the attack.*

DOITA SHIMASHITE – You are welcome.

DOMO ARIGATO – Thank you.

DOMO ARIGATO GOZAIMASHITA – Thank you very much. *At the end of each class, it is proper to bow and thank the instructor and those with whom you've trained.*

DOZO – Please.

ENOY – **Relax.**

FUKUSHIN SHUGO (FUKASHIN SHUGO) – Judge come here! *Call to judges for a conference.*

FUJUBUN – Not enough power.

GEDAN – Lower area of body, groin. *When engaging in Kihon Kumite the attacker will announce his intended target area before executing the attack. This allows the defender the opportunity to prepare for the attack.*

GENKI DESU – I am fine.

HAI – Yes.

172

HAJIME – Begin. *A command given by the instructor or referee to start a drill, Kata or kumite.*

IIE – No, that is incorrect.

IKAGA DESU KA – How are you?

IYEH – No.

JODAN – Upper Area of body, face and head. *When engaging in Kihon Kumite the attacker will announce his intended target area before executing the attack. This allows the defender the opportunity to prepare for the attack.*

KAMAETE – Take up position, fighting stance. *A command given by the instructor for students to get into fighting stance.*

KON BON WA (KON BAN WA) – Hello, good evening. *Greeting after daylight hours.*

KONNICHI WA – Hello, good afternoon. *Greeting during daylight hours.*

KIRITSU (KIREI TU, KIRITS) – Stand, stand up, stand to attention. *Command given by the instructor to stand quickly.*

KI OTSUKE – Attention. *Command given by the instructor to come to attention (Musubi Dachi).*

KUDASAI – Please, if you please.

MATTE – Wait.

MAWATE – Turn. *A command given by the instructor for students to turn around.*

MODOTTE – Return to ready position.

MO ICHIDO – Once again.

MOKUSO (MOKSO) – Meditation. Practice often begins or ends with a brief period of meditation or time out to relax and to compose one's self.

MOKUSO OWARI – Meditation over. *This command marks the end of a period of meditation. Also Mokuso Yame is also used.*

NAO REI – Recover to attention stance. *Command given by the instructor recover to attention and prepare to bow (Musubi Dachi and Rei).*

NA OTTE – Recover. *Generally the command 'Yame' is used.*

NARRA BE NASSAI – Line up.

O HAYO GOZAIMAS (OHIYO GOZAIMASU) – Good morning.

OKEMASU – Stand. *Command given by the instructor to stand.*

ONEGAI SHIMASU (ONIGAI SHIMASU) – I welcome you to train with me, please teach me. *This phrase can be either an offer or a request to train/teach.*

OSS (OOS) – Used as a sign of recognition and respect. *Often used when answering an instructor, bowing at the start and finish of a class and to partners when bowing during kumite. The correct pronunciation is Osu.*

OSWATE – Sit down.

OSU – Greetings. *(See Oss)*

OTAGAI NI REI – Bow to each other, bow to all. *A command given by the instructor for students to bow to one another.*

OTATE – Stand up.

OTOGAI NI REI (OTOGA NI REI) – Bow to all, bow to each other.

O YASAMI NASAI – Good night.

OYASUMI NASAI – Good night. *Used as a departure.*

REI – Bow of respect. *A method of showing respect in Japanese culture is the bow. It is proper for the junior person bows lower than the senior person. Commands to bow: Showmen Ni Rei (bow to the front), Sensei Ni Rei (bow to the teacher), Otagai Ni Rei (bow to each other).*

SAEI REI TU – Line up.

SAYONARA – Good–bye.

SEIRETSU – Line up. *A command given in the Dojo by the instructor, traditionally, senor grades to the right.*

SEMPAI NI REI – Bow to the senior student or students.

SENSEI NI REI – Teacher we bow. *Formal bow to the teacher. This is command given by the Sempai when the students are in a kneeling position at the beginning and end of every lesson.*

SERIDSU – Line up.

SHOBU HAJIME – Start the extended match. *This is a command used by the referee in Kumite competition as he stands on his line.*

SHOBU SANBON HAJIME – Two point completions begin, start the match, begin the bout. *This is a command used by the referee in Kumite competition as he stands on his line.*

SHOMEN NI MUITE – Face the front. *A command given by the instructor for students to face the official seat.*

175

SHOMEN NI REI – Bow to the front, bow to seniors. *A command given by the instructor for students to face the official seat and bow.*

SHUSHIN NI REI – Bow to judges. *A command given by the instructor for students to face the judges and bow.*

SUWARI – Sit.

TATTE – Stand up. *Command to stand up from sitting position.*

TOME – Return to original position

YAMAE (YAME) – Finish, halt, stop, recover, return. *Used by instructors to halt or stop training. Also used by the referee in Kumite competition to interrupt or end a match as he chops down with his hands and the time keeper stops the clock.*

YASUMI (YASUME) – Rest, relax. *A term used by the instructor to tell students to take a relax rest. This is generall in preparation to a drill. Also referred to as Yasunde.*

YOI (YOHI) – Ready, readiness, in a state of alertness. *This is a command to students to come to attention and to go to Yoi Dachi.*

YOI DACHI – Ready stance. *This is the stance taken by karateka when the command "Yoi" is given by the instructor/sensei.*

YUDANSHA NI REI – Bow to a particular, or all, Black Belts.

ZOKKO – Start again, attack, fight. *A command given by the referee for competitors to restart the bout or to urge competitors to attack/fight.*

18

Miscellaneous Terminology (Samazama Na Yogo)

This section contains other useful Japanese words and terminology that may be used in connection Karate training.

様々な用語

ATO DE – Later.

ATERU – To place, to put, to hold.

ATTATE IRU – Contact.

AWASE – Combined.

AWASE WAZA – Combined techniques.

CHADO –The Way of Tea. *The art of the tea ceremony.*

CHIKARA – Power, strength.

CHOKKAKU – Right angle.

CHOKU – Straight.

CHO WA – Harmony. *The combined mental and physical harmony while training.*

CHU – Middle.

DAI – Greater, major.

DAI ICHI – Number.

DOJI – Simultaneous.

EN – Circle.

ENSHIN – Centre of a circle, circular.

FUKAI – Hold strongly.

FUSHO – Injury, wound.

GAMAN – Perseverance, endurance, suffering.

GARAMI – Entanglement.

178

GO:
(1) – Five
(2) – Combat spirit
(3) – Hard – Derives from Goko meaning hard as steel

GOHON – Five techniques, ways etc.

HACHIJ – Eight.

HACHIMAKI – Head wrapping with cloth, head band.

HAN – Half.

HANAJI – Nosebleed.

HARA – The Centre, abdomen, belly. *Also referrred to as Tandan.*

HARU – Spread.

HASAMI – Scissors.

HAYAI – Quick, fast or rapid.

HAYAKU – Quickly.

HENKA – Changing.

HIKKAKU – Scratch, wound with the nails.

HIKUME – Low.

HIRA – Flat, level.

HIRAKU (HIRAKI) – Open.

HON – Basic or fundamental.

HYOSHI – Rhythm.

ICHI:
(1) – One
(2) – Position
(3) – Posture

IMA – Now.

ITCHOKU SEN – Straight line.

ITTAN – Once.

JIYU – Freedom. *As in freedom of movement.*

JOHO – Upward.

JOKO – Slow.

JOKYU – Advanced.

JU:
(1) – Ten.
(2) – Gentle, soft, suppleness, flexibility.
(3) – Hidden source of energy, inside the body. Gentle, soft.

JUJI – Cross.

JUSHIN – Centre of gravity.

KABUSERN – Warp.

KAGI – Hook.

KAHO – Downward.

KAKE – Hooking.

KAMITSUKU – Bite.

KAN:
(1) – Hall.
(2) – Fighting awareness. *To penetrate the true nature of things.*

180

KANI BASAMI – Crab claws.

KANJI – The symbols of Japanese writing. *Of Chinese origins.*

KANSA – Arbitrator.

KAPPO – Resuscitating techniques. Methods of resuscitating those who have succumbed to a shock to the nervous system.

KARA:
(1) – Empty.
(2) – China.

KARIKOMI – Cutting in.

KARUKU – Lightly.

KASEI – Under.

KATA:
(1) – Single, one.
(2) – Form, style, shape, model.
(3) – Shoulder.

KATSU – *See Kuatsu.*

KEGA – Injury, wound.

KIHAKU – Spirit.

KIHON – **Basics, fundamental elementary.** *Basic training or the practice of stances, blocks and striking techniques etc.*

KIRI – Cut, repeat.

KO – Arc.

KOAN – A Zen riddle with no logical answer.

KOKO – Here. Also means 'tiger mouth'. Open hand with fingers together and thumb position to form a 'C' shape with the index finger. Used for attack throat or Adam's Apple.

KOKORO – Spirit, heart. In Japanese culture, the spirit dwells in the heart.

KOKYU – Breath, breathing.

KON BAN WA (KON BON WA) – Good evening. *Greeting after daylight hours.*

KOSA – Cross.

KOWASU – Break.

KU – Nine

KUATSU (KATSU):
(1) – Resuscitating method. *Method for resuscitating one who has lost consciousness due to strangulation or shock.*
(2) – Victory, to win.
(3) – Type of loud shout. *Similar to Kiai.*

KUN – Motto, oath.

KUSSU – Bent.

KUTSU – Pain.

KUZUSHI – Breaking, upsetting.

KYO – Teach, teaching.

KYOKU – Breathing.

KYU – Grade.

KYUSHIN – To study, seek. *Also referred to as Kyoshin.*

MAMA – As it is.

182

MASSUGU –Straight.

MENKYO – License or certificate.

MIGAMAE – Physical readiness.

MIKAZUKI – Crescent moon, new moon. *Also means 'lower jaw bone'.*

MIRU – Look.

MIZU – Water.

MO ICHIDO – Once again.

MOROTE – Augmented, double, two handed.

MOTO – Original.

MUSHIN – No mind. *State of mind where there is no conscious thought.*

MUTSKASAEE – Difficult.

MYAKU – Pulse.

NAGARI (NAGARE NAGAERRU) – Flowing stream, current. *Has the same meaning or translation as Nagashi.*

NAGASHI – Flowing, sweeping.

NAISAN – Man, woman, boy, girl.

NAMI – Wave.

NANAME – Diagonal.

NARABE – Put side by side.

NEKO – Cat.

NI – Two, second.

NIHONGO – Japanese language.

O – Great, major, big.

OKINAWA – The main island of the Ryukyu archipelago.

OKURI – To give back, return.

OREI – Respect, etiquette.

OWARI MASTAH – Over, finished.

REMNEI – Association.

RENRAKU – Combination. *Also referred to as Renzoku.*

ROKU – Six.

RYO – Both.

RYO KEN – Both fist.

RYO KOSHI – Both side.

RYU:
(1) – Way, school, style, method.
(2) – Double. Also means
(3) – Dragon

RYUKYU – The archipelago, group of island, known as Okinawa.

SABI – The term used to describe the feeling one has when finding beauty in a simple, solitary, and perhaps imperfect thing.

SAGI – Heron, crane.

SAKI – Beyond.

184

SAN:
(1) – Three
(2) – Friend. *Used as a suffix to a persons name e.g.*
John San.

SANKAKU – Triangular. *Translates as three angles.*

SASAE – Prop, propping.

SEKAKU – Accuracy.

SHAO LIN – Small forest. *Also Kung Fu method based on eight postures and five animal forms.*

SHI – Four.

SHICHI – Seven.

SHIN – Core, center.

SHIN KEN – Serious.

SHIRO – White.

SHIRYOKU – Eyesight.

SHITEI – Compulsory. *As in compulsory kata in competition.*

SHO:
(1) – Minor, lesser.
(2) – Palm of the hand.

SHOMEN (SHOMON) – Front, forward. *Also means 'front'. 'top of head', 'place of honour', 'founder'.*

SODE – Sleeve.

SOERU – Attach, to attach.

SOESHO – Palm on, palm assisted.

185

SOETE – **Hand on or hand assisted.**

SOKUDO – Speed.

SONO MAMA – As it is.

SOTO – **Outside–inward, outwards, exterior.**

SUIHEI – Horizontal, level.

SUKI – Opening.

SUKOSHI – A little more.

SUMI – Corner.

SUN – Unit of length. *About 3cm.*

SURI – Sliding. As in Hiji Suri Uke or Elbow Sliding Block but is also used to describe when you slide your feet along the floor, Suri Ashi.

TAISO – Callisthenics, exercise.

TAMERAU – Hesitate.

TANDEN – **Centre of gravity, naval area.**

TAOSHI – Down.

TATAMI –Straw floor mat.

TATE – Vertical.

TAIRA NA – Level, even.

TENCHI – Heaven and earth.

TENSHIN SHO – Divine intervention.

TOKUI – Favourite.

186

TOMOE – Circular. *Also means 'stomach'.*

TORA – Tiger.

TSUKKOMI – Charging.

TSURU – Crane, as in the bird.

TSUYOI – Strong, powerful.

UE – Top, above, over.

UCHI – **Inside, inner.** *Also means 'strike', 'strikes', 'striking' and 'inside outward'.*

UKASU – Float.

UKE:
(1) – Receive.
(2) – Block

WA:
(1) – Circle, ring.
(2) – Peace, harmony..

WABI – A sense of loss or loneliness.

WASHI – Eagle.

YASASHEE – Easy.

YAWARA – Control.

YAYA – Slightly.

YAYA ASAKU – Slightly shallow.

YORI – More than.

YOWAI – Weak focus.

187

ZOE – Supporting.

ZENSHIN – Forward or advance.

ZORI – Japanese slippers.

19

Rank
(Dan)

This section contains terminology use with regard to Karateka rank and levels of seniority.

段

DAI SEMPAI – Most senior student.

DAI SENSEI – Great teacher or tenth degree black belt.

DAN:
(1) – Level, rank, degree. *Black belt rank. Also refers to as Danni*
(2) – Man.

DESHI – Disciple, trainee.

DOSHU – Master, master of the way.

GODAN – 5th Dan. *Fifth level/rank/degree black belt.*

GOKYU – 5th grade/level/class of karateka below black belt.

HACHIDAN – 8th Dan. *Eighth level/rank/degree black belt.*

HACHIKYU – 8th grade/level/class of karateka below black belt.

HANSHI – Grand Master 7th to 10th Dan. *An honorary title given to the highest black belt of an organization, meaning wise or sage like and signifying their understanding of their art.*

IKKYU – 1st grade/level/class of karateka below black belt.

JUDAN – 10th Dan. *Tenth level/rank/degree black belt.*

KA – Student, practitioner.

KANCHO – Master of the house, senior instructor of a world wide style.

KOHAI – Junior grade. *A student junior to oneself.*

KOMPAI – Peers, those of similar grade.

KUDAN – 9th Dan. *Ninth level/rank/degree black belt.*

KUKYU – 9th grade/level/class of karateka below black belt.

KURO OBI – Black belt.

KYOSHI – Teacher. *Usually this title is conferred at Rokudan (6th Dan) or Shichidan (7th Dan), depending on system. In large organizations this would be Shichidan (7th Dan). Knowledgeable person or master beyond Renshi but under Hanshi.*

KYU – Boy, Grade. *Signifying achievement below Shodan (black belt).*

MEIJIN – A Great Master, expert.

MUDANSHA – Kyu rank holder. *One without level/grade or students without black–belt ranking.*

NIDAN – 2nd Dan. Second *level/rank/degree black belt.*

NIKYU – 2nd grade/level/class of karateka below black belt.

O SENSEI – Great teacher. Said of Gichin Funakoshi.

RENSHI – One who has mastered oneself. *An expert instructor or master a name usually awarded to a 5th Dan (Godan), depending on the system.*

ROKKYU – 6th grade/level/class of karateka below black belt.

ROKUDAN – 6th Dan. Sixth *level/rank/degree black belt.*

SANDAN – 3rd Dan. *Third level/rank/degree black belt.*

SANKYU – 3rd grade/level/class of karateka below black belt.

SEITO – Pupil, student.

SEMPAI – A senior grade student. *The literal translation is mentor, sponsor, patron.*

SENSEI – Teacher, one who has gone before. *It is usually considered proper to address the instructor during practice as "Sensei" rather than by his/her name. If the instructor is a permanent instructor for one's Dojo or for an organization, it is proper to address him/her as "Sensei" off the mat as well.*

SHICHIDAN – 7th Dan. *Seventh level/rank/degree black belt.*

SHICHIKYU – 7th grade/level/class of karateka below black belt.

SHIDOIN – Assistant instructor. *Formally recognized instructor who has not yet be recognized as a Sensei.*

SHIHAN – Instructor, teacher, expert, master. *High ranking coach 6th Dan (Rukudan) and above. A formal title meaning, master instructor or teacher of teachers. Also referred to as Shinan.*

SHODAN – 1st Dan. *First level/rank/degree black belt.*

SHOMEN (SHOMON):
(1) – Place of honour. Also includes the designated front of a dojo. *Traditional etiquette prescribes bowing in the direction of the designated front of the dojo whenever entering or leaving the dojo.*
(2) – Founder. Literal translation is 'first head'.
(3) – Also means 'front', 'forward', 'front of top of head'.

TAISHO – Leader, captain of the team. *Also means 'palm heel'. The palm of the hand when the fingers are drawn back. Also referred to as Shotai and Shotei.*

UCHI DESHI – Number one student, aapprentice, inside student, live–in student. *A student who lives in the dojo and is devoted to training, maintaining the dojo and serving the Sensei.*

YODANSHA (YUDANSHA) – One who is a black belt, black belt holder of any rank.

YONDAN – 4th Dan. *Fourth level/rank/degree black belt.*

YONKYU – 4th grade/level/class of karateka below black belt.

YUDANCHA – The collective name for all Dan grades present.

YUDANSHA (YODANSHA) – One who is a black belt, black belt holder of any rank.

YUDANSHAKAI – Group of black belt holders.

20

The Dojo Kun

This section contains the translation of the Dojo Code of conduct for Shotokan Karateka and what perhaps should be the essence of the motivation and morality of all martial arts.

道
場
訓

THE DOJO KUN

Hitotsu! Jinkaku Kansei Ni Tsutomuru Koto!
One! To Strive For The Perfection of Character!

Hitotsu! Makoto No Michi O Mamoru Koto!
One! To Defend The Paths of Truth!

Hitotsu! Doryoku No Seishin O Yashinau Koto!
One! To Foster The Spirit of Effort!

Hitotsu! Reigi O Omonzuru Koto!
One! To Honour The Principles of Etiquette!

Hitotsu! Kekki No Yu O Imashimuru Koto!
One! To Guard Against Impetuous Courage!

It is generally believed that the principles of the Dojo Kun
were passed down by Okinawan martial arts masters and
the exact wording was later formalist by Gichin Funakoshi.

Seek Perfection of Character
Defend the Path of Truth
Endeavour to Excel
Display Courtesy
Refrain from Violent Behaviour

Master Funakoshi said:

**"The ultimate aim of Karate-Do lies neither in
victory nor defeat, but in the perfection of the
character of its participants".**

196

21

The Twenty Precepts (Karate Do Niju Kun)

This section contains Gichin Funakoshi' s
20 Precepts or Guiding Principal written to assist
students to develop spiritually and mentally.

空手道二十訓

1   Karate begins with courtesy and ends with courtesy.

2   There is no first attack in karate.

3   Karate is an aid to Justice.

4   First control yourself before attempting to control others.

5   Spirit first, technique second.

6   Always be ready to release your mind.

7   Accidents arise from neglect.

8   Do not think that Karate training is only in the dojo.

9   It will take your entire life to learn Karate; there is no limit.

10   Put your everyday living into Karate and you will find Myo (The subtle secrets!).

11   Karate is like boiling water. If you do not heat it constantly, it will cool.

12   Do not think that you have to win, think rather that you do not have to lose.

13   Victory depends on your ability to distinguish vulnerable points from invulnerable ones.

14   The battle is according to how you move guarded and unguarded (move according to your opponent!).

198

15 Think of your hands and feet as swords.

16 When you leave home, think that you have numerous opponents waiting for you.

17 It is your behaviour that invites trouble from them.

18 Beginners must master low stance and posture; natural body positions are for the advanced.

19 Practicing a Kata is one thing, engaging in a real fight is another.

20 Do not forget to correctly apply: strength and weakness of power, stretching and contraction of the body and slowness and speed of techniques.

Always think and devise to live the precept every day.

22

Counting In Japanese
1 -100
(Nihongo No Kazoe)
(Ichi Kara Hyaku Made)

This section contains the translation of the numbers one to one hundred from English into Japanese.

日本語の数え
一から百まで

1-50

1	ICHI	26	NI JYU ROKU
2	NI	27	NI JYU SHICHI
3	SAN	28	NI JYU HACHI
4	SHI	29	NI JYU KU
5	GO	30	SAN JYU
6	ROKU	31	SAN JYU ICHI
7	SHICHI	32	SAN JYU NI
8	HACHI	33	SAN JYU SAN
9	KU	34	SAN JYU SHI
10	JYU	35	SAN JYU GO
11	JYU ICHI	36	SAN JYU ROKU
12	JYU NI	37	SAN JYU SHICHI
13	JYU SAN	38	SAN JYU HACHI
14	JYU SHI	39	SAN JYU KU
15	JYU GO	40	YON JYU
16	JYU ROKU	41	YON JYU ICHI
17	JYU SHICHI	42	YON JYU NI
18	JYU HACHI	43	YON JYU SAN
19	JYU KU	44	YON JYU SHI
20	NI JYU	45	YON JYU GO
21	NI JYU ICHI	46	YON JYU ROKU
22	NI JYU NI	47	YON JYU SHICHI
23	NI JYU SAN	48	YON JYU HACHI
24	NI JYU SHI	49	YON JYU KU
25	NI JYU GO	50	GO JYU

51–100

51	GO JYU ICHI	76	SHICHI JYU ROKU
52	GO JYU NI	77	SHICHI JYU HICHI
53	GO JYU SAN	78	SHICHI JYU HACHI
54	GO JYU SHI	79	SHICHI JYU KU
55	GO JYU GO	80	HACHI JYU
56	GO JYU ROKU	81	HACHI JYU ICHI
57	GO JYU SHICHI	82	HACHI JYU NI
58	GO JYU HACHI	83	HACHI JYU SAN
59	GO JYU KU	84	HACHI JYU SHI
60	ROKU JYU	85	HACHI JYU GO
61	ROKU JYU ICHI	86	HACHI JYU ROKU
62	ROKU JYU NI	87	HACHI JYU SHICHI
63	ROKU JYU SAN	88	HACHI JYU HACHI
64	ROKU JYU SHI	89	HACHI JYU KU
65	ROKU JYU GO	90	KYU JYU
66	ROKU JYU ROKU	91	KYU JYU ICHI
67	ROKU JYU SHICHI	92	KYU JYU NI
68	ROKU JYU HACHI	93	KYU JYU SAN
69	ROKU JYU KU	94	KYU JYU SHI
70	SHICHI JYU	95	KYU JYU GO
71	SHICHI JYU ICHI	96	KYU JYU ROKU
72	SHICHI JYU NI	97	KYU JYU SHICHI
73	SHICHI JYU SAN	98	KYU JYU HACHI
74	SHICHI JYU SHI	99	KYU JYU KU
75	SHICHI JYU GO	100	HYAKU

203

ISBN 141209342-2

Printed in Great Britain
by Amazon